FREE
TRADE
the real story

free traders usually cite the General Agreement on Tariffs and Trade (GATT) as the alternative on which Canada should rely.

The GATT has served Canada well since World War II and Canadians who believe in free trade also believe in the GATT. Indeed, the two are quite complementary since the Canada-U.S. FTA is consistent with the GATT.

The problem with the GATT from a Canadian point of view is that it is on a four- to five-year negotiating timetable. That is too long for Canada to wait, given the imminent threat of more U.S. protectionism. Furthermore, there is precious little assurance of a GATT breakthrough.

This is because the United States is quite legitimately insisting that other countries reduce their agricultural and service sector barriers if the United States is not to raise its manufacturing barriers. Canada fully supports this U.S. demand, particularly in relation to agricultural commodities. The problem is that powerful vested interests — particularly among farmers in western Europe and Japan — may be too strong to permit these countries to make the kinds of concessions that are required.

The advantage of free trade with the United States for Canada is twofold in the GATT context. In the first place it provides an example for the world that could help to break the GATT logjam. At the same time it provides a hedge against any possible breakdown in the GATT negotiations.

The positive case for free trade with the United States should be obvious. The United States represents the single wealthiest market on the face of the earth. More ready and secure access to that market can provide Canada with an opportunity that will be the envy of the rest of the world. This is all the more important since Canada does not appear to have the competitive strength to export large volumes of manufactured goods to any other country.

The latter point undermines the argument that free trade will turn Canadians into hewers of wood and drawers of water. The reverse is actually the case, since the United States is the only country to which Canada now exports a significant amount of manufactured goods. Even if the United States is deemed to represent an economy in secular decline — an unsubstantiated claim at best — it will remain a lucrative market for Canadian producers for the foreseeable future.

The arguments in favor of free trade with the United States are basically economic in nature but they have obvious non-economic ramifications. This is because it is only through the economic growth and prosperity that free trade can help produce that Canada can generate the wherewithal to finance more generous cultural, regional-development, and social-security programs.

Most of those who favor the FTA feel just as strongly about these programs as anyone else. Unlike many others, however, they worry about how these programs are to be paid for, particularly if Canada loses any more access for its products and services to its major foreign market than it already has.

The Case Against Free Trade

Both valid and not-so-valid arguments have been raised against the Canada-U.S. FTA. Perhaps the most legitimate or at least logical reason for opposing free trade is the one that is largely unstated in the ongoing debate over the issue. There are those who oppose free trade because they favor more state intervention in the economy. They think that the prospects for such intervention will be diminished by Canada having closer economic ties with a country like the United States, which is so committed to a competitive enterprise market system.

On a non-ideological, philosophical, or political basis the most valid argument against free trade pertains to the job disruption that will occur due to free trade, minimal as that disruption may be relative to other ongoing shifts in the labor market. Although studies reviewed later in this book demonstrate that Canada will gain more jobs than it loses because of free trade, there will be a few losing as well as many winning firms, industries, and sectors.

The inevitable manpower disruptions caused by free trade are likely to represent a fraction of the shifts that are continually taking place in the labor force. Nevertheless, there will be the need for adjustment assistance for those forced to change jobs so that these workers are not forced to bear the costs for benefits that accrue to all Canadians.

Much less valid concerns have been expressed about the impact of free trade on everything from Canada's culture, through the country's regional-development programs and social-security systems, to its very sovereignty — if not its very existence. These concerns persist despite strong reassurances to the contrary.

For example, culture has been virtually exempted from the terms of the FTA, except for one or two relatively minor provisions. Also, no mention is made in the agreement of regional subsidy programs, although these remain countervailable unless modified in the next round of negotiations over a code of fair-trade behavior between the two countries. Social-security programs are in no way covered by the FTA. Canada's sovereignty is bound to be affected by any treaty the country signs, but on balance, Canada's sovereignty may well be enhanced by this particular one if only because of the FTA's dispute-settlement provisions.

All of these concerns are so contentious that they warrant individual treatment later in this book. This is the only way to demonstrate clearly how much they have been distorted and exaggerated by the anti-free-trade forces.

Outline of this Book

Appropriately, this book begins with a chapter that details the historical background of the current free-trade initiative. This is followed by a description of the negotiating process that led to the present agreement.

The next seven chapters deal with key components of the agreement: tariffs, services, agriculture, the auto pact, energy, foreign direct investment, and dispute settlement. Among the questions answered are

- What did Canada gain?

- What did Canada not gain?

- What did Canada give up?

- What did Canada not give up?

- What are the critics and opponents saying?

- Why are the anti-free traders wrong?

The next four chapters consider some of the key adjustments made necessary by free trade, as well as the assistance that may be required to cope with its implementation. Highlighted are the implications of the FTA for business, the employment effects of free trade, and its impact on women.

Chapters 14 and 15 cover consecutively the equally sensitive issues of social policy — education, regional development, and social security, and some critical dimensions of sovereignty. It is vital that Canadians understand how little has been conceded in these vital areas.

Then, three other important facets of the FTA are examined: the constitutional issues involved, the relationship of the Canada-U.S. FTA to the GATT, and a U.S. perspective.

The Conclusion draws on all of the preceding material to bring out the major misconceptions and misrepresentations that exist in relation to the Canada-U.S. FTA. This agreement is too vital to Canada's future well-being to allow these misconceptions and misrepresentations to persist.

CHAPTER 1

Canada's Historic Search for Secure Markets

What did Canada's first prime minister, Sir John A. Macdonald, have in common with Canada's current prime minister, Brian Mulroney? And what did these two Conservatives have in common with Liberal prime ministers Alexander Mackenzie, Sir Wilfrid Laurier, and William Lyon Mackenzie King? The answer to both questions is that, at one time or another, they all supported some form of free trade with the United States.

Almost every Canadian government has consistently pursued better trade relations with the United States and greater access to U.S. markets. They knew that Canada's relatively small population made it necessary to secure foreign markets to keep production costs low and Canadian products competitive. And they all knew that the facts of geography and similar economic and political values and systems placed the U.S. market front and centre for Canada. The history of Canadian commerce has been a history of attempting to fully exploit the tremendous opportunities that the U.S. market has always offered, while at the same time searching for the widest possible offshore markets.

Canadian commercial interests and farmers first clamored

David J. Bercuson is Professor of History, University of Calgary. He specializes in modern Canadian political, diplomatic, and defence policies, post-1940.

for a trading agreement with the United States in the early 1850s. Canada's fragile economy had been jeopardized by Britain's rapid movement toward free trade the decade before. The Industrial Revolution had given the British the world's most powerful economy. British businessmen wanted to abolish tariffs altogether so that they could buy the raw materials they needed as cheaply possible. As long as those tariffs existed, however, the products of British colonies had been given preference over those of non-British countries. When the tariffs were abolished, British-Americans were forced to compete in the British market on the same terms as everyone else. They were unable to do so. In 1849, Tory businessmen in Montreal clamored to be annexed to the United States, where a growing new market beckoned. But when a dispute over U.S. access to Canadian coastal fishing grounds blew up shortly after, the Canadians were able to negotiate a reciprocity or free-trade treaty in natural products with the United States in exchange for U.S. access to Canadian fish. This was Canada's first trade agreement with the United States.

The 1854 Reciprocity Treaty solved Canada's search for wider markets for a time. A thriving trade grew in natural products such as fish, grain, and rough lumber between the British-American colonies and the United States.

Canadians did not, of course, give up on Britain or the Empire. Britain remained Canada's largest trading partner until well into the twentieth century, and access to the massive British market was still the main prize to be won. At the same time, Canadian manufacturers began to demand tariff protection for their fledgling industries and were rewarded with an upward revision of customs duties by the colonial government in 1859. Virtually no one in the Canada of the mid-nineteenth century saw an inconsistency between seeking freer trade with the United States and greater trade with Britain while, at the same time, trying to protect certain key sectors of the economy.

In 1864 the United States gave notice that it wanted the

Reciprocity Treaty to end in 1865. The government in Washington was now dominated by high-tariff Republicans who were unhindered, in those Civil-War days, by low-tariff southern Democrats. Republican power increased even more with the final victory of the Union in the spring of 1865. For the next five decades the U.S. Congress was ruled by men representing the manufacturing interests of the northeast and the mid-west who scoffed at the notion of trade treaties with tiny Canada.

The Canadians, however, kept trying. One of the main reasons for the creation of the new Dominion of Canada in 1867 was to establish a wider free-trade area among the former colonies, to mitigate the ending of reciprocity. However, the re-establishment of reciprocity was a major political objective of both Macdonald's Conservatives and the Liberals. During negotiations in Washington in 1871 to settle a range of outstanding British, Canadian, and U.S. issues, Macdonald tried once again to trade access to Canadian fish for a reciprocity agreement. But the United States was not interested.

In November 1873 a scandal forced Macdonald to resign from office. The Liberals under Alexander Mackenzie were elected early the next year. The Liberals favored lower tariffs in principle. However, they assumed office at the start of a long depression and soon raised tariffs slightly when government coffers ran low due to depressed trade (there was no income tax in those days). They too tried to cajole the United States into another reciprocity agreement. They too failed.

Macdonald regained power in 1879 by promising to raise tariffs to protect Canadian industry. The country was still mired in depression and Macdonald's policy of economic mastery looked a lot better to most voters than Mackenzie's policy of economic drift. The first budget of the new Conservative government created a comprehensive tariff structure designed both to protect existing industries and to stimulate the founding of new ones. This was the National Policy tariff and it became a basic part of Canada's economic system until at least the 1930s. It was also, the Liberals were to learn in two elections, the closest thing Canada had to Mom and Apple Pie.

The National Policy tariff was a mixed blessing for Canada. There was tremendous growth in Canada's industrial sector, with the iron and steel industry reaping particular rewards. Thousands of new jobs and hundreds of new millionaires were created. But industries were also established that had no rhyme or reason for being in Canada in the first place — except that some entrepreneur saw a National Policy-created opportunity. A large textile industry grew up in Quebec and Ontario, for example, even though no cotton ever grew in Canada. A Canadian rubber industry was also born. Some of these industries existed only because of the tariff, not because there was a natural market in Canada for their product. They were and still are inefficient, subsidized by the government through tariffs and other means, and paid for by consumers through higher prices.

Macdonald championed higher tariffs after 1879, but he saw no inconsistency between his National Policy and reciprocity in natural products with the United States. Indeed, when he first raised the idea of a National Policy tariff in the House of Commons in 1878 (while still leader of the Opposition), Macdonald had declared that such a tariff, by "moving ... in the direction of a reciprocity of tariffs with our neighbours" would "tend to procure for this country, eventually, a reciprocity of trade." Therefore, when a new dispute over fisheries arose in late 1884 and early 1885, Macdonald angled for another reciprocity agreement with the United States — an agreement that would supplement his National Policy tariffs. Once again he failed and a third attempt in 1891 failed also.

Macdonald wanted reciprocity in natural products with the United States but he did not want across-the-board free trade. Canada was not ready for that in the late nineteenth century in any case. Although U.S. markets grew rapidly after the Civil War — and Canadian trade with the United

States grew as well — Britain was still Canada's major trading partner. Besides, Macdonald sincerely believed that Canada could eventually build an economic structure to rival that of the United States in size and power. That meant smokestack industry and continued protection, whatever the costs to Canadian consumers and farmers. To him, it was a necessary condition of Canadian survival, just as the Canadian Pacific Railway was. Therefore, Macdonald hitched the fortunes of the Conservative party to the manufacturers and businessmen of Canada.

That became obvious in the 1891 federal election when the Liberal party, now led by Wilfrid Laurier, campaigned on a platform of "unrestricted reciprocity with the United States." This was too much for Macdonald and for a majority of Canadian voters who believed — or who were led to believe by Macdonald — that such a policy would lead to annexation. Their fears were fed by indiscreet Americans who tried to rally support for the cause south of the border by claiming that such a policy would mean the eventual expansion of the United States to the Arctic Ocean. Macdonald wrapped himself in the Union Jack with his cry of "A British subject I was born, a British subject I will die" — and won the election.

In those days, when the British Empire was reaching its zenith and when a large proportion of "English" Canada had been born in the British Isles, the appeal to British patriotism was strong. When Laurier contested the 1896 federal election, he made sure that Canada's business leaders knew that he had abandoned unrestricted reciprocity and now stood squarely behind the National Policy. He was elected; the National Policy remained.

Although a clamor for free trade with the United States grew in western Canada as hundreds of thousands of pioneers settled the land after 1896, Laurier had other problems to solve — the creation of Alberta and Saskatchewan, the building of a new transcontinental railway, defining Canada's relationship with Britain. But reciprocity, at least in natural products, still beckoned. In 1910 Laurier had his chance.

Canadian trade negotiators went to Washington in late 1910 when a trade dispute with the United States loomed on the horizon — the United States resented Canada charging lower tariffs on British goods than on U.S. goods. There the Canadians found a new political climate. Progressive political forces were vying for power with the old-style Republicans and a new mood seemed to prevail. To the surprise of the Canadians, the United States offered a comprehensive reciprocity agreement in natural products with certain other tariff concessions on a very limited list of manufactured products, mainly agricultural.

The U.S. Congress passed the reciprocity agreement in July 1911, but Laurier faced stiff opposition in the House. Stymied by a Conservative filibuster, Laurier called an election even though he had more than two years left in his mandate. He went to the people in September and lost. The Conservatives won by a landslide: 134 seats to the Liberals' 87.

In the years since the 1911 election, the myth evolved that when the Canadian people had cast their ballots, they had spoken clearly and loudly against free trade with the United States. On closer examination, this is simply not true. Laurier also lost the election because of major Liberal defeats in Quebec, where the dominant issue was not reciprocity but whether or not Canada should build its own navy. In fact, the popular vote across Canada was very close — the Conservatives won 51.2% of the vote while the Liberals won 47.8%. Nevertheless, the free-trade issue appeared settled, at least for the moment. Although Canada and the United States concluded two broad trade agreements in the 1930s, neither aimed at free trade.

Throughout the twentieth century Canada has imported more from the United States than it has from Britain, but in 1942 Canadian exports to the United States outstripped those to Britain for the first time. Since then the United States has been Canada's most important trading partner, despite periodic efforts by some Canadian prime ministers (e.g., Diefenbaker, Trudeau) to diversify Canadian trade. Canada most keenly felt the impact of that change in the trading relationship immediately after World War II, when free trade came to the fore once again.

Canadians went on a buying spree after Hitler's defeat. Wage controls, rationing, and wartime shortages ended, and the future looked bright for the first time since the Great Depression began in 1929. Soldiers returned from Europe, got married, and began to raise families. The baby boom — and a tremendous postwar expansion — began.

The boom caused a bust of Canada's dollars holdings. Most of the things Canadians wanted to buy, from radios to cars, were manufactured in the United States. The rush to buy produced a massive dollar outflow because, at the same time, Canada was earning much less from foreign trade than it usually did. Canada's traditional overseas customers, particularly Britain, had been ruined by the war. Canada was spending much more than it was earning. The government began to consider tough measures such as currency controls to combat the problem. In the late fall of 1947 Ottawa slapped heavy restrictions on imports.

In an effort to solve the problem, Canada approached the United States in late October 1947 to propose a comprehensive free-trade agreement. This was in keeping with the belief that had developed in Ottawa during the war that Canada should aim to liberalize foreign trade as much as possible after the fighting was over. This impulse had made Canada a strong supporter of the General Agreement on Tariffs and Trade, the International Monetary Fund, and the World Bank.

Over the next several months, Canadian and U.S. negotiators, meeting in great secrecy, worked out an agreement that would have established a modified customs union between the two countries. This was a far more comprehensive agreement than the abortive reciprocity agreement negotiated in 1911. At first, Prime Minister William Lyon Mackenzie King strongly supported the initiative, but by early March 1948 he was having second thoughts. By the end of the month, he had made up his mind that Canada must not go ahead. On April Fool's Day in 1948 Canada informed the United States that the deal was off.

Why did King kill the agreement? According to his diary, King backed out when he concluded that free trade with the United States would destroy the unity of the British Empire and open him up to Conservative charges that he had sold Canada out to the United States. By that time it was becoming increasingly apparent that Canada was forging a new continental defence relationship with the United States, and this new relationship was making some Canadians, particularly those of Conservative stripe, very nervous. Adding free trade would have been 1911 all over again, and King had been a great admirer and follower of Laurier.

The death of the 1947–48 free-trade relationship was not, of course, the end of the Canadian-U.S. trading partnership. Trade between the two countries has continued to increase while a number of sectoral free-trade agreements have been signed. The most famous of these is the auto pact, agreed to in 1965. But talk of across-the-board free trade did not revive until the recent Macdonald Commission hearings.

Much has changed in Canada since the Reciprocity Treaty of 1854, the 1911 general election, or the uncertain days of the late 1940s. Now it is the manufacturers who most want free trade, while many farmers are reticent. Now it is the Liberals who oppose free trade even though the Liberal party has traditionally been its major supporter. But one overall factor remains as it did in 1948, in 1911, and earlier: there are those Canadians, confident of the future and of their identity as Canadians, who seek to expand trade across the globe but who also want to compete as equals in the U.S. market. And there are still those who, out of fear, wave the flag and shout jeremiads about the future of a Canada linked in free trade to the United States. They are certain as their forebears were that Canada is a fragile country that will not be able to resist the siren call of total immersion in the Great Republic. Times and the faces have changed, but the message remains the same.

CHAPTER 2
The Negotiating Process

In 1985 the prime minister of Canada and the president of the United States, first at the Shamrock Summit in Quebec City and then through the formal exchange of letters launching the negotiations, espoused a common vision: the removal of barriers to trade between their two countries. When it came time to translate these objectives into an agreement, however, the two governments set about their task in very different ways.

The reasons were obvious. The U.S. agenda was already overcrowded with issues ranging from the trivia of a presidential candidate's sex life to the critical questions of war and peace, leaving the "Canada agreement" to struggle for attention in the special-interest politics of Washington.

The stakes were very much higher in Canada, where the initiative was the focus of unremitting media attention as the centrepiece of the government's economic development strategy. As the only industrialized country without free access to a major consumer market, Canada's prospects for diversifying from excessive dependence on volatile international resource-commodity markets hinged on enhanced and secure access to her giant neighbor to the south.

Ambassador Gordon Ritchie is Deputy Chief Trade Negotiator for Canada, Trade Negotiations Office, Ottawa.

The Canadian Team

On the Canadian side a brand-new organization was established — the Trade Negotiations Office (TNO) — with responsibility for both the bilateral and multilateral negotiations. It was headed by Canada's best-known trade negotiator, Simon Reisman, architect of the Canada-U.S. auto pact, whose vast experience dates back to his role on Canada's delegation to the founding meetings of the General Agreement on Tariffs and Trade (GATT) in 1947. Reisman brought to the negotiations two indispensable elements: a profound commitment to a classical free-trade area, and a reputation as a scrapper who would stand up for Canada's interests.

Reisman was joined by two experienced deputy ministers, Dr. Sylvia Ostry, the internationally respected former deputy minister of trade, had particular responsibility for the Uruguay Round of multilateral trade negotiations. I came back from Toronto to help with the preparations for the bilateral negotiations.

The TNO management cadre was composed of outstanding individual performers in their own right. Alan Nymark came direct from the Macdonald Commission, whose report he had largely authored and which strongly favored free trade. Germain Denis, from the trade department, had established his credentials as a highly experienced international trade negotiator over the past two decades. Charles Stedman came from the industry department, where he had spearheaded negotiations with the automotive industries of three continents. Andrei Sulzenko had worked closely with Reisman on an earlier automotive task force, and now managed the difficult issues of services and investment. An invaluable late addition to the team was general legal counsel, Konrad von Finckenstein, Q.C., the top trade lawyer in the justice department.

The rest of the team was hand-picked from the top experts from within the Canadian public service and from outside practice. On tariffs, for example, the director of the tariffs division of the finance department was seconded to the TNO; on agriculture, the department of agriculture seconded the top agricultural trade expert; on trade in services, the director of the responsible office in the industry department joined the team; on U.S. countervail laws, one of the top lawyers from the Washington trade bar was retained to support the TNO's general counsel. In all, some forty senior professionals were brought on strength, backed up by top-notch support staff and the latest in computer systems. The team was directly accountable through Reisman and myself to the Trade Executive Committee of Cabinet, chaired by the prime minister or the deputy prime minister.

Other ministers and their departments were also heavily involved. Critical issues were discussed in the full Cabinet and in the Priorities and Planning Committee. The responsible deputy ministers met biweekly under my chairmanship to review progress in the negotiations. Their staffs were heavily involved in the preparatory work. The final responsibility at the negotiating table, however, rested squarely with the TNO.

After a rocky start at a First Ministers' Conference in Halifax in the fall of 1985, the provincial governments became deeply involved in the process, short of actually sitting at the negotiating table. Every month, Reisman chaired daylong sessions with the designated senior trade representatives from the ten provinces and two territories to review the negotiating positions. The premiers themselves, while keeping their freedom to manoeuvre, were extensively briefed in three regular First Ministers' Conferences and eight special meetings on the trade negotiations, meetings that often ran for eight hours or more. At the end of the process, seven premiers came out in favor of the arrangement, three were opposed, but all had been closely consulted.

Perhaps most importantly, the Canadian business community was highly supportive and deeply involved from the beginning. The initiative had, indeed, originally been urged on the government by the leadership of big and small business alike — the Business Council on National Issues, the Canadian Manufacturers' Association, the Canadian Chamber of Commerce, the Canadian Federation of Independent Business, and others. Once the negotiations were underway, we made the decision to tap into this support and knowledge to a precedent-setting degree. An International Trade Advisory Committee, under the able chairmanship of Walter Light, former chief executive officer of Northern Telecom, provided overall advice on matters ranging from the negotiating mandate through to adjustment issues. Fifteen sectoral advisory groups were established to give more focussed advice on the major industries involved. These business leaders were brought into the negotiators' confidence and consulted closely on everything from the detailed phasing of tariff reductions on specific items through to an overall position on investment policies. More than 250 men and women were involved, from right across the country.

The one regret was the absence of organized labor participation, with the notable exception of the Canadian Federation of Labour. The rest of the labor movement staked out an early position in adamant opposition to the whole idea, which precluded their open involvement in the process, although extended private consultations were occasionally possible.

In sum, Canadian preparations were painstaking and highly professional. Based on consultations with industry advisors and provincial officials, positions were developed by the TNO. These comprised a broad overall mandate, followed by specific mandates in each of the major subject areas of the negotiations. These were then reviewed with federal departments through my committee of deputy ministers and submitted for decision to the Cabinet. The agreed position was then reviewed with the provinces. Finally, a well-prepared position was presented to the U.S. representatives at the negotiating table. Progress was continuously reported back to the federal, provincial, and business participants in the process.

As a result, I believe that when the Canadian team came to the negotiating table, we were as well prepared and as highly supported as any team in Canadian history. We needed to be. What the U.S. representatives lacked in preparation and organization they more than made up in sheer economic clout. The United States controlled what Canada needed most — access to a giant consumer market. The strategy was simple: in return for access to that market, under U.S. rules and on U.S. terms, the Canadians would have to accommodate a long list of U.S. concerns, identified by special-interest groups and retailed to the U.S. Administration through congressmen and senators. To protect Canadian interests and achieve our key objectives, the Canadian team would have to mobilize the best resources we could muster.

The U.S. Team

On the other hand, this power imbalance largely explains the very different approach the United States took to organizing its side of the negotiations. Sheer economic strength could offset what U.S. representatives lacked in detailed support. Their preparations could take place far from the glare of media, or indeed congressional attention, until the final culmination of the negotiations.

To co-ordinate these preparations, Peter Murphy was brought back from his post as ambassador to the GATT in Geneva and given one officer and one secretary to do the job within the office of the U.S. Special Trade Representative. For his technical support he was largely dependent on the good will of the various departments whose powers he would be trading away. The International Trade Commission had to advise on any change in tariffs. The Department of Commerce had to approve any move involving trade-remedy laws. The Department of Agriculture jealously retained its prerogatives when it came to farm products. The U.S. Treasury, of course, insisted on having the final say on all matters in its jurisdiction. These departments and agencies assigned middle-ranking officers to work with Murphy on a part-time basis.

Predictably, the U.S. team had little or nothing to do with the individual states, beyond the occasional briefing of governors' staffs. More surprising, the team received relatively weak support from the U.S. business leadership, whose attention was focussed on domestic issues and on the protectionist omnibus trade legislation working its way through the Congress. A year and a half after the start of negotiations, the Advisory Committee on Trade Negotiations (the U.S. equivalent of the International Trade Advisory Committee) had not yet given any priority to the Canada-U.S. Free-Trade Agreement (FTA).

Closing the Deal

From the official launch in April of 1986 through the summer of 1987, the two teams under Reisman and Murphy struggled with the complexity of putting together the biggest trade deal ever concluded between two countries. Three-day sessions were held, alternating between Canada and the United States, on a monthly basis to begin with, then accelerating to biweekly and, at the end, almost weekly meetings. At each meeting a number of subjects were tackled. Initially one side or the other would prepare a full negotiating proposal and make an opening presentation. After the other side had reflected and delivered its response, working groups were established to find the facts and narrow down the issues. Laboriously, the pieces were slowly assembled into an overall package as the relatively straightforward issues were resolved, leaving a residue of seemingly intractable differences. The secret negotiating sessions between the two teams were a striking counterpoint to the Canadian-media glare of publicity surrounding the talks. The U.S. media continued largely to ignore the negotiations.

Under these circumstances, and given the importance of the arrangement, it is hardly surprising that escalation to the political level was ultimately required to close the deal. During eighteen months of intensive negotiations the two teams had explored all the major issues in the negotiations and identified the acceptable solutions for most. Indeed, by September of 1987 an "integrated model agreement" had been assembled that incorporated the work of both teams. There remained, however, a number of specific irritants of particular political concern to the U.S. team and there was lack of agreement on the critical issue to the Canadians: the binding settlement of disputes over subsidies and dumping. The "crunching" of these issues required three days of high political drama in Washington to meet the deadline for the U.S. negotiating authority.

The "Elements of Agreement" were finally concluded on October 4, 1987, and officially released to the public on the following day. (An earlier U.S. "Synopsis" was actually released on the previous day, but was riddled with errors and wishful U.S. thinking.) It took two more months of intensive work before the legal text of the FTA could be tabled by the prime minister in the House of Commons, in both official languages, running to nearly 3 000 printed pages. Finally, on January 2, 1988, in parallel ceremonies, the prime minister in Canada and the president in the U.S. signed the final legal text of the FTA. This agreement will form the basis for implementing legislation to be presented to Parliament and to the Congress with the objective of getting approval in time for the FTA to enter into force at the beginning of 1989.

CHAPTER 3
Tariffs and Other Border Measures

Canada is a small country dependent on international trade for its prosperity. Almost 30% of Canadian gross national product is generated directly by exports. Between 70% and 80% of those exports go to the United States — the exact figure varies with world trading conditions. So access to foreign markets is critical to Canada's well-being.

The main purpose of the Canada-U.S. Free-Trade Agreement (FTA) is to improve Canada's access to the market of its most important trading partner. This is seen not as a substitute for the multilateral pursuit of access through the next round of the General Agreement on Tariffs and Trade (GATT) negotiations, but as a complement to it. However, in practice, most GATT observers expect a much larger increase in access to come from the FTA than from the GATT.

For almost sixty years Canada's infant industries developed behind the high tariff walls of the National Policy, which was first introduced in 1879. Then, in 1935, Canada

Richard G. Lipsey is Senior Economic Advisor, C.D. Howe Institute, Toronto. **Robert C. York** is a policy analyst for the Institute. Further recommended reading on border measures are R.G. Lipsey and M.G. Smith, *Taking the Initiative: Canada's Trade Options in a Turbulent World* (Toronto: C.D. Howe Institute, 1985), and Victoria Curzon Price, *Free Trade Areas, The European Experience: What Lessons for Canadian-U.S. Trade Liberalization?* (Toronto: C.D. Howe Institute, 1987).

embarked on a course of gradually reducing tariffs to inte-grate Canadian industry into the world economy. This policy served Canada well over the next fifty years. During that time nearly 80% of trade barriers were dismantled, while Canadian industry prospered and employment, foreign trade, and real incomes grew. Now, the FTA represents an attempt to remove most of the remaining trade barriers. It is thus not a new initiative, but rather it is the near-culmination of a policy that has seen most Canadian industries grow from sheltered children in the 1930s to healthy adults in the 1980s.

Trade liberalization means the removal of border restric-tions. The FTA also contains some special conditions to con-strain the misuse of the so-called fair-trade laws that can become potent non-tariff barriers (NTBs) in the form of countervail and anti-dumping duties. In fact, countervail and anti-dumping duties have attracted most of the attention in the Great Debate over the FTA. However, the bulk of the increase in access to the U.S. market will come — and would come even in a perfect arrangement that removed all barriers of all types — from the reduction in border measures. These are measures that remain *permanently* in place to restrict trade, in contrast to such *temporary* measures as anti-dump-ing and countervailing duties, which are imposed to deal with specific problems and then are removed. Desirable though it would be to constrain the use of these temporary measures, this would provide an increase in access much smaller than the increase that will follow from the removal of the permanent border measures.

It is to these border measures, largely ignored in the Great Debate, that this chapter is devoted.

What Canada Agreed To

Both countries agree to remove *all* bilateral border measures on trade in goods ten years after the FTA comes into force. This includes tariffs, tariff-related measures, quantitative restrictions, and other restrictive measures that impede the free flow of trade.

All remaining tariffs are to be phased out over a ten-year transition period beginning on January 1, 1989 (Article 401). Where industry representatives requested it, the duties will be phased out over a five-year period, or removed completely in January 1989. These tariff cuts can be accelerated whenever both sides agree.

The United States applies a customs user fee to all imports into that country, equal to 0.17% of the value of the imported product. This is a direct trade impediment and will be eliminated in 1994.

The FTA confirms our GATT rights and obligations relating to import and export restrictions on two-way trade, including the use of NTBs (Article 407). The FTA removes unilateral import and export restrictions such as quotas, minimum-price requirements, and taxation measures that discriminate on the basis of nationality. Exceptions are allowed only for well-defined purposes such as supply shortages, conservation, national security, or the enforcement of countervailing and anti-dumping laws (Articles 407 and 409).

Two measures that have been much used in the past to distort trade patterns are to be eliminated. Duty drawbacks — the practice of refunding to domestic producers the duties levied on materials imported from third countries when they are subsequently processed into exported goods — are to be phased out by 1994 (Article 404). Duty remissions (or waivers) — the practice of refunding import duties in return for requiring production and/or employment guarantees — will be removed by 1998 (Article 405).

Export taxes on goods shipped to the other party are prohibited (Article 408). Any other export restrictions can be justified as long as these are consistent with GATT measures, but only if the imposed restriction

• does not reduce the proportion of the total supply of the

restricted good that the other party received before the restriction was put in place

- does not impose higher prices for exports to the other party through licences, fees, taxes, or minimum-price requirements

- does not require the disruption of normal supply channels (Article 409)

These conditions, which have caused much debate, are intended for use in rare cases of severe shortage (which situation can be declared to exist at the sole discretion of the exporting country).

In essence, the FTA makes the GATT measures more explicit and, without question, more enforceable, ensuring that these rules will no longer be ignored, as now happens under the GATT supervision. GATT supporters should welcome this aspect of the FTA as giving real effect to principles of which they approve.

What Canada Gained in Terms of Access

What Canada gained from the FTA can be divided into two categories:

- most obviously, those elements specific to the FTA

- less obviously but no less important, those benefits that result from a liberalized trading environment

Consider the specific elements first. Perhaps the two most significant achievements in the FTA are the clear and stringent rules of origin (chapter 3 of the FTA) and the right of national treatment (chapter 5). The clear rules of origin remove any ambiguities as to which goods qualify for preferential treatment; they specify exactly the rate of tariff on all goods; and they effectively exclude the trans-shipments of goods from third countries through one country into the other, thus ensuring that the benefits of free trade go only to the partners in the deal. The only exception to the provision that allows full duty-free access to goods that meet the rules of origin is for apparel made in Canada or the United States. For these goods, annual quotas are established for duty-free treatment, quotas that are set well above the current levels of trade.

The national treatment obligations (Articles 501 and 502) establish the principle of equal treatment of equals. This is no small gain, since discriminations based on national origin, for example, by sales or excise taxes, or more onerous health and safety measures, have often been used to put Canadians at a competitive disadvantage.

Canadians gain from the removal of some significant NTBs. First, there will be more generous access to government procurement and a mutual prohibition of any actual or disguised forms of trade barriers. Canada also gains relief from U.S. protectionist or retaliatory measures aimed at others — the so-called sideswipe problem. Many U.S. trade actions directed at Japan, the European Community, and Asian newly industrializing countries have sometimes caught Canada in the crossfire, since U.S. laws apply equally to all foreign jurisdictions. The FTA prevents this from happening.

Second, consider the broader economic benefits of liberalized trade. Customs duties erode domestic purchasing power and reduce product choices. Since we are all consumers, we are all affected. Removing the tariffs lowers both domestic and import prices, and this means more purchasing power in the hands of all of us.

Producers gain the opportunity to rationalize production plans to accommodate higher volumes of exports, not only to the United States but also to the rest of the world. Cost savings will accrue through scale economies and increases in productivity that will make domestic firms more competitive internationally.

Often overlooked is the gain from heightened competition. The FTA will help unleash competitive forces that improve the economy's dynamism. Competition induces the use of the most cost-effective inputs and production processes. It also encourages capital and labor to move from sunset to sunrise industries, and most importantly, it invites firms to move quickly into new product mandates to serve the enlarged market.

What Canada Did Not Gain in Terms of Access

In terms of tariff removal, Canada gained all that it wanted. Furthermore, the FTA gives more control over NTBs than any other trade agreement — so on this score Canada gets more from the FTA bilateral negotiations than it could possibly hope to bargain for on a multilateral basis.

What Canadian negotiators did not get, and would have liked, is access to U.S. transportation markets and a subsidy and anti-dumping code for trade remedies (all of which are matters of NTBs). The issue of trade-remedy laws is handled in a later chapter of this book. On transportation, Canada did not gain access to maritime shipping (protected in the United States by the Jones Act) nor to continental trucking. This is a big disappointment since these markets are lucrative.

What Canada Gave Up

What Canada gave up to get the FTA signed has been the focus of much of the free-trade debate. On border measures, both sides gave up rights whose sacrifice is the essence of a free-trade area, no more and no less. Each party relinquished the right to erect trade-restraining measures that arbitrarily or unjustifiably discriminate against the nationals of the other country. In a world where Canadians are concerned to maintain the principles of fair trade, this cannot be seen as a concession. So whatever price Canada paid to get the advantages of a significant increase in market access is in areas beyond border measures, areas that are discussed in other chapters of this book.

What Canada Did Not Give Up

In terms of border measures, Canada did not give up

- controls over the export of raw logs

- controls over the exports of unprocessed east-coast fish

- controls over the sale and distribution of beer

- the right to maintain and expand the use of supply-management regimes in agriculture (e.g., marketing boards)

- the right to use emergency measures in case of a surge in imports as a result of bilateral free trade or global emergency actions

Although it represents victories at the bargaining table, this list does not represent an unmixed blessing for Canadian consumers.

Canada did not give up the right to implement any policy that it deems to be in its best interests. The FTA removes many trade barriers but it does not regulate social policies, nor, with a few exceptions, does it regulate economic policies other than those that restrict the free flow of trade. (For details see chapter 15, "Sovereignty".) Further, Canada's ability to pursue independent trade policies with any other country is preserved.

What the FTA Critics and Opponents Say

The following is a sampling of the tariff-related objections to the FTA.

Objection: Canada has more to lose from tariff elimination, since its average level of tariffs exceeds that in the United States.

Response: Nothing can be further from the truth. Because Canada's average tariff level is higher, this country has more to gain when tariffs are removed. The farther tariffs fall, the greater are the price reductions for consumers, and the more room there is for rationalization of production by producers.

Objection: Removing tariffs does not eliminate regional disparities.

Response: Free trade with the United States is no panacea, and regional inequalities will no doubt persist. However, with free trade, a redistribution of income in favor of the have-not provinces should occur, as provinces that import manufacturing goods find their prices falling.

Objection: Canada cannot compete tariff-free with the United States.

Response: This one sounds like a last-ditch effort to strike fear into the hearts and minds of Canadians. Canada *can* compete with the United States. It is no accident that organizations representing large, medium-sized, and small Canadian business support free trade. They know they can compete.

Objection: Canada's high-cost, high-wage economy cannot trade freely with the low-cost, low-wage U.S. economy.

Response: The mechanism that allows any two countries to trade, whatever their domestic cost levels, is the exchange rate. If the United States were to produce all goods at lower cost than Canada, Canadian consumers would opt to consume all U.S.-made goods. To pay for the U.S. products, Canadians would demand U.S. foreign exchange. The U.S. dollar would then be bid upward, making Canadian imports less expensive in terms of U.S. dollars, and U.S. imports more expensive in terms of Canadian dollars. When the exchange rate settles down, mutually beneficial, two-way trade occurs.

Objection: The FTA means that U.S. protectionism becomes Canadian protectionism.

Response: This allegation was commonly heard earlier in the debate. Because it sets up a free-trade area, not a customs union, there is nothing in the FTA regulating trade barriers against third countries. Canada is free to establish its own independent commercial policy in relation to third countries.

Objection: Canadian industry will be forced to compete tariff-free with goods that are produced by third countries (particularly those made in Mexican plants located near the U.S. border) and then enter Canada through the United States.

Response: The clear statement of rules of origin effectively rules out this allegation, which has gained wide circulation.

Objection: The FTA does not guarantee a significant improvement in Canadian access to the U.S. market.

Response: The following is a list of the ways in which the FTA improves Canadian access to the U.S. markets. Let the reader judge if the objection carries weight.

- By embedding the rules of the GATT into innumerable clauses throughout the FTA, these rules, which are designed to encourage market access, are given greater enforceability.

- Clear rules of origin remove all of the uncertainty currently associated with ad hoc decisions of customs officers as to what tariff is payable on specific items as they cross the border (Article 301).

- All tariffs will be eliminated on all trade with the United States by 1998 (Article 401).

- The threat of quantitative restrictions used to force countries to adopt voluntary export restrictions (VERs), is removed (Article 407).

- The right of national treatment protects Canadian producers from discrimination by the United States on all activities covered by the FTA (Article 501).

- Various NTBs, such as standards requirements, are eliminated (Article 603).

- Tariffs will be removed on all agricultural goods, as well as quotas, except when they are used to support supply management (as in poultry and eggs) (Articles 401 and 702).

- Free trade is established for red meats (Article 704).

- The FTA grants significant exemptions from U.S. restrictions on importing Canadian food products containing sugar (Article 707).

- Canadian energy products are given secure access to the U.S. market and shielded from the U.S. threat of countervail — this is notably the case in relation to oil and gas, enriched uranium, and electricity (Articles 902 and 905).

- Short of a shooting war, national security can no longer be used to restrict exports of Canadian energy products to the United States as was commonly done in the United States before the first Organization of Petroleum Exporting Countries (OPEC) oil shock, and is currently being discussed in relation to all oil imports into the United States (Article 907).

- The auto pact was not gutted, so free trade in automotive goods is secure and entrenched, and cannot be upset without abrogation of the entire FTA (Article 1001).

- The uncertainty caused by escape-clause action (which was used, for example, against shakes and shingles) is reduced to a minimal level.

- Canada is freed from U.S. global actions aimed at others — the so-called sideswipe problem is removed (Article 1102).

- Some government procurement markets are opened up (Article 1304).

- Free trade is established for a wide range of service industries (Articles 1401 and 1402).

- The easy granting of temporary entry to the United States of Canadian business people and service personnel removes a major barrier to the sale of many products (Article 1501).

- Assured access is promised to financial markets when U.S. (Glass-Steagall Act) laws are amended (Article 1702).

- The dispute-settlement procedure will make the application of U.S. trade laws less political and, by shortening the appeal process, will make redress from bad decisions easier (Article 1904).

- Consultations designed to revise countervail and anti-dumping laws are mandatory over the next seven years (a degree of close consultations that we would be highly unlikely to be able to maintain without the FTA) (Article 1907).

To turn down this impressive list of improvements in access because Canada did not get even more by agreeing on a code for subsidies and anti-dumping seems to be letting the best be the enemy of the good — with a vengeance.

Conclusions

The case for bilateral free trade with the United States is strong. In accepting it, Canadians are not plunging into uncharted waters. The FTA is in every way, without exception, like the GATT. The spirit and provisions of the bilateral treaty are patterned after its multilateral cousin. There are no surprises. The FTA simply takes this country farther and faster than it will be able to travel along the multilateral route — which is not, in any case, foreclosed by the FTA.

CHAPTER 4
Services

Many people seem to be mystified by the services aspect of the Canada-U.S. Free-Trade Agreement (FTA), particularly because the United States took the initiative in relation to this issue. This chapter is intended to answer the following questions.

What is involved in trade in services? Why has it become an important international issue? What provisions are contained in relation to trade in services in the FTA? What trade-offs were made in the negotiations? What are the implications for future Canadian and U.S. policies?

What Is Trade in Services and Why Does It Matter?

The term "trade in services" can be defined in many ways. However, for our purposes this phrase can be defined simply as the international exchange of intangibles (services) that have value to producers or consumers.

People tend to think of services in terms of the personal services used by households. However, apart from services

Murray G. Smith is Director of the International Economics Program, Institute for Research on Public Policy, Ottawa. This chapter draws on longer papers by the author, including "Services and Investment Issues in the Canada-U.S. Free Trade Agreement" by J. Schott and M. Smith, presented at a conference in Washington, January 11, 1988 and forthcoming in *The Canada-U.S. Free Trade Agreement: A Time for Decision*, to be published jointly by the Institute for International Economics and the Institute for Research on Public Policy; and "Canada in the Word Services Economy: Economic and Policy Issues," by M.G. Smith, an unpublished manuscript.

provided by restaurants and hotels, most services that are traded internationally are services to business, such as engineering, transportation, accounting, advertising, financial, and data processing services.

Trade in services perhaps can be best understood by contrasting it with trade in goods or tangible commodities. International trade in goods, whether it is in primary commodities such as wheat or lumber, or high-technology products such as computer chips and compact disks, involves items that can be counted or measured by customs officials at a border. It may be hard to determine the value of a computer chip or a compact disk, but at least in principle, the existence of the product can be readily verified when it crosses international boundaries. In contrast, trade in services involves intangibles and it is often difficult to determine when or if an international transaction has occurred.

Conceptually at least, trade in services is also distinct from investment flows or income from foreign investments. Direct trade in services involves some immediate production activity and therefore is akin to trade in goods because it is linked to current employment and economic activity, while investment flows or income from investment reflect savings from past economic activities or past transactions.

Of course, policy issues involving trade in services are often closely linked to investment issues or immigration issues. Some services, such as data processing, can be offered across national borders simply by dialing up via long-distance telephone lines. Other services, however, require investment in local distribution facilities or the relocation, at least for a short time, of specialized technical personnel.

Trade in services has emerged as a policy issue because of economic and technological factors. Due to continuous improvements in the technology — and dramatic reductions in the costs — of transportation and communications, the potential for international exchange of services is expanding rapidly. Twenty-five years ago a manufacturing firm would have relied on its local accountant and bank manager to provide financial services. Today, manufacturers obtain those services from the global service industries that have developed. A manufacturing firm that lacks, or is denied, access to global accounting, consulting, and financial services can be severely inhibited in its ability to compete as a manufacturing enterprise.

Therefore, trade in services involves competition from abroad for domestic-services industries that may not have faced this competition in the past. At the same time, global competition in the services industries can be an important element in the competitiveness of the goods-producing economy.

What Was Agreed On in the FTA?

The key element in the FTA pertaining to trade in services is a commitment by both countries to national treatment in all new policies. National treatment means that foreign and domestic firms are treated the same under laws and government policy. This means that all of the existing discriminatory practices are grandfathered and can be maintained or renewed, unless there is a specific provision in the FTA that curtails the discriminatory practices. In future, however, governments must abide by a commitment to national treatment in specific services industries that are covered under the FTA.

The FTA provisions apply only to specific services industries. These include a broad range of business and consulting services to the resource and manufacturing industries, as well as insurance, real estate, and wholesale distribution. In addition, there are specific sectoral agreements that apply to tourism, architects, and computer services and data transmission.

Major services sectors are explicitly excluded from the provisions of the FTA. The major excluded sectors are the cultural industries, the transportation industries, and basic telecommunications services. Various other services, such as day-care, health services, education, and other social services also are not covered under the services provisions. Thus, not only can existing discriminatory policies affecting all these services industries be retained and new, non-discriminatory regulations be imposed, but also new discriminatory regulatory, tax, or subsidy measures can be imposed by either country.

In addition to sectoral exclusions, the obligations under the FTA do not apply equally to all policy instruments. Services are explicitly excluded from the commitment to eliminate procurement preferences, except for some trade-related services already covered under the General Agreement on Tariffs and Trade (GATT) procurement code. There are no restrictions on the provision of subsidies to services industries and there is a vague commitment that tax measures will not discriminate excessively. Finally, differential treatment can be justified for "prudential, fiduciary, health and safety or consumer protection reasons."

Perhaps the most important achievement of the FTA in relation to services is the provision facilitating business travel. Temporary entry by business visitors, traders, professionals, and intracompany transfers will be liberalized between Canada and the United States, but there are no changes in either country's immigration policies regarding establishment of permanent residence. Not only will it be easier for a Canadian engineer to work on a construction project in the United States, but it will be easier for a Canadian manufacturing firm to install and service specialized equipment sold to U.S. customers. However, the temporary-entry provisions will not apply to entertainers and performing artists. Both countries have restrictive temporary-entry regulations now, but U.S. restrictions have been particularly troublesome recently.

The obligations under the FTA impinge on areas of provincial jurisdiction in Canada and also on some state practices in the United States. The FTA enjoins both federal governments "to take all necessary measures" to ensure that local governments comply with the FTA, which is a stronger commitment than the "all reasonable measures" language in the GATT.

Since existing discriminatory practices are grandfathered, no changes in provincial or state policies are required to implement the FTA, but future actions of provinces or states will be subject to scrutiny under the general dispute-settlement mechanism in the agreement.

Indeed, all of the FTA commitments in relation to services are subject to the agreement's general dispute-settlement procedures, with one notable exception. Financial services are dealt with separately from other services industries and are not subject to the dispute-settlement provisions.

The agreement on financial services covers commercial banks, securities dealers, and trust and loan companies, which are subject to federal regulation. In most respects, the financial-services agreement continues the gradual trend toward deregulation in financial markets that both governments have pursued. Both governments commit to liberalize their financial markets, to extend the resulting benefits to the firms of the other country, and to establish a consultative mechanism to oversee the liberalization. As with the entire financial-services pact, the consultative mechanism is not subject to the dispute-settlement provisions of the FTA, and is to be administered by the U.S. Treasury and the Canadian Department of Finance. Furthermore, unlike the other services, there are no provisions regarding regulatory policies at the state or provincial level.

The FTA will free U.S.-owned banks and other financial institutions operating in Canada from some current restrictions on market share and asset growth. In particular, U.S. commercial bank subsidiaries will not be subject to the 16% ceiling set by the Canadian Bank Act on the foreign bank share of the total domestic assets of all banks in Canada, and restrictions on the establishment of intra-Canada branches by U.S.-owned Schedule B banks will be removed. Moreover, national treatment will be accorded to new applications from U.S. commercial banks to enter the Canadian market. In addition, the limits of 25% total foreign participation in Canadian Schedule A banks will be dropped for U.S. nationals or firms under the FTA. The 10% ceiling for individual holdings regardless of nationality still remains, however, for the Schedule A banks. Similarly, formal ownership restrictions are being removed for federally regulated insurance and trust and loan companies. Many of the changes in Canadian policy would probably occur in the next review of the Bank Act. The most dramatic development in Canadian financial policies has been the unilateral move by the Ontario government to open provincially regulated securities dealers to foreign ownership. But Ontario's move was independent of the trade negotiations and the FTA financial-services provisions do not apply to provincial policies.

The FTA includes important commitments to safeguard the extensive U.S. business operations of Canadian banks and allows them to underwrite Canadian government securities in the U.S. market. It is noteworthy that Canadian financial holdings in the United States are about four or five times greater than U.S. financial holdings in Canada. The FTA guarantees the right of Canadian banks to retain the multistate branches grandfathered under the International Banking Act (IBA) of 1978. Since the IBA is subject to review after ten years, the FTA provides safeguards that the multistate banking privileges of Canadian banks will be retained. The FTA also guarantees Canadian financial institutions national treatment under prospective amendments to the Glass-Steagall Act. Since the securities industry is subject to federal regulation in the United States, Canadian financial institutions are obtaining greater certainty about the future evolution of U.S. securities policies than U.S. firms are obtaining about Canadian policies.

What Were the Tradeoffs?

Reaching agreement on the coverage of the services provision involved difficult negotiating tradeoffs. On the Canadian side there was great reluctance to consider any policy commitments that would limit the measures used to support the cultural industries. On the U.S. side there was considerable pressure to obtain some reductions in the degree of discrimination in Canadian cultural policies that impose burdens on influential lobbies in the United States. Canada also was reluctant to consider national treatment commitments in service activities such as day-care, nursing homes, and other personal services, but U.S. negotiators found this to be less contentious.

While Canadians argue cultural sovereignty, Americans argue national security as grounds for excluding services industries from the FTA. In particular, U.S. maritime interests mounted a strong and effective lobby to protect the Jones Act and other existing or prospective measures to support the U.S. merchant marine, which they argue is vital to U.S. national security. Although the Canadian shipping industry was keen to obtain access to U.S. coastal shipping, the sentiment of the Canadian airline, trucking, and rail interests was mixed.

The result of these lobbying pressures on both sides of the border was that there were extensive sectoral exclusions from the services agreement. Canada did not get the access to the U.S. transportation sectors that it sought, but Canada was able to retain a panoply of cultural-support policies affecting trade in goods and services.

What Are the Policy Commitments?

The policy commitments on services trade are widely interpreted as placing serious constraints on the formulation of Canadian policies. The policy constraints are more limited than most people appreciate, because of sectoral exclusions, such as cultural industries, transportation, basic telecommunications, and a variety of social services; because of policy exemptions such as procurement preferences and subsidies; and because new regulations can be justified on "prudential, fiduciary, health and safety or consumer protection" grounds.

The commitment to national treatment is frequently misunderstood in popular commentary on free trade. For example, media reports have referred to an Ontario government study that concluded that the FTA would require dismantling of the Ontario Film Censorship Board. In fact, there is nothing in the FTA that would affect the operation of the Ontario Film Censorship Board. If the Ontario board passed a policy that stated films made in Ontario were not subject to censorship because of the higher moral standards of filmmakers in that jurisdiction but that films made outside of the province were subject to censorship requirements, then that would be contrary to national treatment. Nevertheless, that policy would not be an issue under the provisions of the FTA but it would be a violation of the rules under the GATT for trade goods that apply to films.

Under the FTA the capability of Canadian governments, whether federal or provincial, to regulate domestic and services industries or to promulgate new standards for services industries is unconstrained, if those regulations are for domestic-policy purposes and are not applied in a discriminatory fashion. The belief that an agreement on trade in services will require harmonization of domestic regulatory policies reflects this fundamental confusion about the meaning of a national treatment obligation. National treatment means that foreign firms and domestic firms engaged in the same activity are treated the same way under domestic law in the domestic market. National treatment does not require that the foreign firms must receive the same treatment in the domestic market as they receive in their home base of operation. Yet that is what many of those who are concerned about policy harmonization presume in their concern about the effects of the FTA.

Service activities that are excluded under the FTA, such as day-care, nursing homes, the provision of certain educational services, or other social services, not only can be subject to non-discriminatory regulations in future, but also they can be subject to explicitly discriminatory regulations. Thus, a foreign company proposing to operate a day-care centre could face tougher licencing standards in relation to its facilities or the qualifications of personnel that it employed, while Canadian firms or non-profit day-care operations could be exempted from these requirements and receive special subsidies.

In addition, the FTA permits the establishment of new monopolies established by governments to provide either services or goods to domestic consumers. Thus a provincial government that does not presently have a public auto-insurance monopoly could institute such a monopoly in the future. The only restriction on the operation of such a provincial monopoly in the services industries would be that the monopoly could not compete unfairly, or engage in predatory practices, in other markets that were not subject to the monopoly designation. For example, a provincial automobile-insurance monopoly could not use profits from its captive automotive customers to subsidize its competition with commercial firms providing casualty insurance. This is an extension of the competition laws that both countries apply to predatory pricing practices and monopolization.

It is clear that the FTA precludes certain discriminatory policies by either country in selected services industries. For example, Canada is committing not to impose restrictions on the amount that Canadian tourists are allowed to spend in the United States. Although Canada runs a bilateral deficit on the tourism account, Canadians will have to judge for themselves whether this and similar provisions in the FTA are undesirable policy commitments.

Conclusions

The primary achievement of the FTA in relation to services is to prevent the introduction of new discriminatory policies while only limited progress was made in rolling back barriers to trade in services. Perhaps the most significant trade-expanding policy change is the easing of restrictions on business travel. In areas such as financial services the FTA consolidates recent trends toward more open and competitive markets for Canadian services industries.

The constraints placed on Canadian policies in relation to services are less severe than many people imagine. Canada's capability to pursue a broad range of domestic-policy goals is unaffected. Both countries have agreed, however, to avoid discriminatory and protectionist actions in the business services sectors.

Most importantly, the FTA will create a new and more stable environment for bilateral economic relations. The FTA establishes, for the first time, clear contractual obligations on Canada and the United States in relation to services trade. These obligations are subject to an expeditious, rule-oriented, dispute-settlement mechanism. These innovations will provide a more predictable environment for the private sector to plan its business strategies, and will help to facilitate the resolution of disputes between the federal governments.

Clearly the services provisions of the FTA have been shaped by national sensitivities on both sides and by unique stresses on the world's largest bilateral commercial relationship, but negotiating these elements of the FTA provide useful experience and precedents for the multilateral negotiations in the Uruguay Round. The FTA achieves less in rollback of existing barriers to services trade and investment than some might have hoped, but the selective liberalization and focussed obligations under these provisions offer guidance for multilateral efforts to develop rules and dispute-settlement mechanisms for services trade and investment issues.

Over the decade ahead, Canadian services industries will be challenged to find their vocation in the emerging global services economy. In turn more competitive Canadian services industries will enhance the competitiveness of Canada's resource and manufacturing industries.

CHAPTER 5
Agriculture

Agrifood was a particularly difficult sector for both countries to include in the Canada-U.S. Free-Trade Agreement (FTA) for three reasons:

- the sector is subject to extensive economic and technical regulation

- the most heavily protected subsectors are politically very influential

- the major problems in agricultural trade (e.g., the use of subsidies and quantitative import restrictions) can only be dealt with satisfactorily in the multilateral negotiations being conducted in the General Agreement on Tariffs and Trade (GATT)

Nevertheless, agriculture and food trade had to be included, because each country had specific export interests to promote and both realized that the exclusion of agriculture by two such important exporters would have sent entirely the wrong signals to Geneva.

During the FTA negotiations, agriculture and wines and distilled spirits were the subject of detailed sector-specific agreements. The agreement on liberalizing trade in farm and food products can be characterized as broad but not deep.

T.K. Warley is Professor of Agricultural Economics, University of Guelph. He is currently engaged in research on agriculture in relation to the GATT multilateral trade negotiations as well as for the Canada-U.S. FTA. His latest publication is the forthcoming *Agricultural Protectionism in the Industrialized World* (Washington, D.C.: Resources for the Future).

44

Its numerous specific elements individually and collectively provide for a significant measure of agricultural trade liberalization, but neither country was ready to eliminate entirely the frontier measures and within-border assistance programs that shape agricultural food production and trade.

Gains

Improved access to the U.S. market for a broad range of Canadian farm and food products exports is provided by the agreement to phase out all tariffs over a ten-year period, by the exclusion of Canada's beef exports from the quantitative restrictions of the U.S. Meat Import Law and by the exemption of Canada from any future quantitative restrictions imposed by the United States on grains. Further improvements in access will result from successful implementation of agreements to ban the use of technical regulations as concealed protection, to work toward the harmonization of regulations and standards, and to accept the equivalence of national inspection and certification systems.

Canadian agricultural and food exporters also approve of the FTA provisions that will provide more assured and predictable access to the U.S. market. In particular, hog and cattle producers, meat packers, and other groups that have been the target of U.S. countervail, anti-dumping, and safeguard actions, believe that the dispute-settlement provisions of the FTA will enhance objectivity in the application of the remedy provisions of U.S. trade law, act as a deterrent against frivolous trade complaints, and permit Canada to influence future U.S. trade legislation.

The Canadian products that are expected to benefit from improved and assured access to the U.S. market include wheat, oats, canola and soybean oils and meals, cattle and hogs, beef and pork cuts, processed meat products, beans, potatoes, carrots, onions, rutabagas, cole crops, mushrooms, some flowers, pot plants and nursery stock, and myriad individual processed food products ranging from pasta to quality wines. Happily,

Canada has a large number of entrepreneurs who can benefit from these improved market opportunities.

Shortfalls

The major area in which the bilateral accord on agriculture came up short was in the failure to come to grips with the direct and indirect subsidies to agricultural production that are the root cause of trade distortions in agriculture. The two countries were not able to agree on a definition of what types of government-assistance programs constitute trade-distorting (and hence countervailable) subsidies, and to write new rules to govern their use and the response to them (e.g., higher standards of proof of injury and causality, higher levels of injury, and acceptance of the principle that only the net difference in national subsidies should be countervailed). The design of new trade laws on subsidies (and anti-dumping and safeguards measures) will be addressed bilaterally in the period to 1994 and, in practice, this task may well be left to the multilateral GATT negotiations now in progress.

There *were* some agreements on agricultural subsidies — not to use export subsidies in bilateral trade, to be mindful of the other country's legitimate trade interests when using export subsidies in offshore trade, and to withdraw the rail transportation subsidy on Canadian exports to the United States shipped through west-coast ports. Also, Canada will open its market only to U.S. exports of wheat, barley, and oats, and their products, when national grain-support levels are equal. But these measures will not affect the massive support being given to agricultural production and export in the United States — particularly to grains — that are helping to depress world grain prices and thereby imposing huge costs on Canadian farmers and taxpayers.

Sacrifices

Since people tend to measure their standard of living by

what they consume rather than by what they produce, economists do not perceive the contraction of uncompetitive industries as a result of trade liberalization as a loss. Nevertheless,
it is customary to judge the results of trade arrangements, in
part, by counting the protection surrendered in the reciprocal
exchange of concessions. And, certainly, industries and firms
that lose protection will face a reduction in incomes and asset
values and other adjustment costs.

In this light, the major concessions in agriculture and food
that were made to the United States were

- the phase-out, over a ten-year period, of the tariffs that
  provide protection to some parts of the horticultural and
  food-processing industries

- the termination of the procurement, mark-up, and domes-
  tic-content practices followed by provincial liquor boards
  that discriminate against U.S. wines and grapes

- the conditional elimination of import licences on U.S.
  exports of wheat, barley, and oats and related products

- a one-time increase in Canada's import quotas for poultry
  meats and eggs to the import levels actually achieved in
  the previous five years

The removal of horticultural tariffs will have some adverse
effects on the producers of tender fruits and vegetables for
both the fresh market and for processing. Indeed, in large
measure, processors will offset the loss of tariff protection in
food products that they will experience by exerting downward pressure on the prices they pay for the fruits and vegetables they use as ingredients. Similarly, wineries will pay less
for grapes. And grain-using industries will be able to meet
tariff-free competition in flour and bakery products only by
paying competitive prices for wheat. This will require the
replacement of the two-price wheat scheme under which
Canadian wheat growers have been able to charge approximately twice the world market price for wheat used for

human consumption in Canada. The increase in the import
quotas for U.S. shipments of eggs, chickens, and turkeys
translates directly into a small loss of market share for egg
and poultry-meat producers and for the packers and processors of these commodities. Additional losses would occur if
imports of further-processed egg and poultry products were
permitted to increase as a result of tariff removal.

Hence, other things being equal, the FTA implies some
reductions in prices, revenues, incomes, asset values, output
and market shares for some producers of fruits, vegetables,
grapes, and "feather" products, and some negative economic
effects for wheat growers and some parts of the Canadian
food-processing industry. Of course, other things will not be
equal; all manner of market adjustments and policy changes
will be made that will help these sections of the agrifood
system accommodate to increased competition.

Retained Protection

Negotiators on agrifood from both countries were charged
with the avoidance of some outcomes. Therefore, neither the
United States nor Canada was able to offer in a bilateral
negotiation the large concessions on agricultural subsidies
and import controls that may later be required — and be
more valuably made — in a global accord on agriculture that
includes the European Economic Community and Japan.
Specific Canadian imperatives were to retain two agricultural policy instruments: stabilization and marketing boards.

The decision to postpone the quest for a new code of trade
conduct means that the issue of whether payments under
commodity stabilization programs constitute countervailable
subsidies is unresolved. Accordingly, Canada's Agricultural
Stabilization Act 1975 and Western Grain Stabilization Act
1976 are unaffected by the bilateral FTA.

Canada's marketing boards were never an issue as such,
any more than were U.S. marketing orders and agreements.
What was at stake were the import controls that are the

underpinning of the pricing and market-control programs of some boards operating in the Canadian market. Where trade arrangements have changed, the powers of the relevant boards have changed also, or appropriate policy adjustments have had to be made.

There is no change whatsoever in the operation or market power of agency boards such as those in place for hogs. Negotiating and price-setting boards for such farm commodities as fresh and processed fruits and vegetables and grapes will have the ceilings lowered on the prices they can get for growers as a result of the tariff-free access to the Canadian market of U.S. raw farm products and processed foods and wines. However, the boards can continue to perform exactly the same range of functions as before. Similarly, although the Canadian Wheat Board (CWB, a Crown corporation) and the Eastern grain-producers' marketing boards, will be unable to extract a premium price from Canadian buyers of wheat once U.S. grains and grain-based food products can be imported without licences and tariffs, respectively, nothing has changed the "orderly marketing" powers at home and abroad of the CWB and the provincial grain boards. Furthermore, the danger that Canadian grain-grading and quality-control systems would be compromised has been averted by the requirement that imported U.S. grains be accompanied by end-use certificates, consigned directly to final buyers, and be denatured if for feed use.

Finally, and most importantly, the formula-pricing and supply-control programs operated in Canada for fluid and industrial milk, shell eggs, chickens, turkeys, and hatching eggs for broilers are left essentially intact since the FTA provides explicitly for the continuation of quantitiative import controls in support of present (and future) national supply-management programs. To be sure, import quotas for eggs and poultry meats have been expanded, but only by amounts equal to about 1% of domestic production. Domestic producers are still guaranteed 94% to 98% of the Canadian market. Nor will these shares be eroded by the importation of tariff-free, further-processed products, because government has promised to put such products on the import control list, should rising imports threaten to undermine domestic-pricing arrangements and Canadian producers' market shares.

In the case of the formula-pricing and supply-management arrangements for milk, the embargoes on imports of liquid milk and dairy substitutes were grandfathered, no increases were granted in the quotas of products now under quantitative import restrictions, and at the insistence of milk producers and dairy processors, products previously excluded by tariffs were placed on the import-control list within days of the FTA being signed. Hence, it is arguable that the made-in-Canada arrangements for producing, marketing, and pricing milk are more secure than before the FTA was signed.

Conclusions

Opponents of the FTA have focussed their criticisms on three aspects of its agrifood components:

- the harm done to particular subsectors as a result of removing protection

- the surrender of national autonomy in policymaking for the Canadian agricultural and food system

- the weakness of the mechanisms created to ensure secure access to the U.S. market

Some subsectors and firms in the Canadian agrifood system will unquestionably be disadvantaged by the loss of protection. However, major negative effects will be concentrated in a very narrow segment of the industry, namely, some fruits and vegetables, grapes and wine, and some processed foods. For the remainder of the industry, the salient features of the FTA are the retention of protection for the most highly regulated sectors — milk and poultry — or the creation of huge additional market oportunities by opening the U.S. market to competitive Canadian producers of grains, oilseeds, red meats, some horticultural products, and some processed foods.

By any calculus, for the agricultural sector as a whole, the economic gains outweigh the losses. Moreover, while it is true that negative effects will be concentrated in Ontario and Quebec, the magnitude of these losses has been manifestly overstated. Thus, the estimate of a loss of $95 million in gross revenue to Ontario farmers was arrived at only by counting potential losses that will not in practice occur (e.g., the revenue lost from the termination of the two-price wheat plan is to be paid by other means, and the threatened influx of tariff-free dairy and poultry products will not be permitted), and by a relentless pessimism about the ability of Ontario farmers and food manufacturers to benefit from enlarged opportunities in the U.S. market.

Additionally, it has been too readily assumed that loss of protection would result in the disappearance of affected sub-sectors. This is unlikely. To be sure, there will be some reductions in profitability, some devaluation and change in ownership of assets, and difficult adjustments for some people and firms. It may be necessary to compensate for these losses and assist adjustment. But there is absolutely no reason to expect that, for example, fruit and vegetable or grape and wine production will cease, and output may not even contract.

In an integrated market, trading partners must avoid using policy instruments that could lead to charges that competition is not fair. In this sense, there is necessarily some loss of sovereignty in the creation of a free-trade area. However, it is hard to sustain the charge that the FTA has seriously constrained Canada's ability to assist Canada's farmers and food processors or to pursue other goals for the agrifood system. Key instruments of Canadian agrifood policy — stabilization, marketing boards, formula pricing, and supply management — are intact, and there is nothing in the FTA that would compromise Canada's high standards in plant and animal health or the quality and safety of Canadians' food supply.

Finally, agricultural critics of the FTA have complained that it does not give Canadian producers the assured access to the U.S. market that the proponents of the FTA had promised. If these critics mean that Canada will not be exempt from the remedy provisions of U.S. trade law, the response must be that Canada was not prepared to volunteer the disciplines on the use of subsidies and marketing practices that such an exemption would have entailed, nor would Canadian producers have been comfortable with a reciprocal exemption for the United States from Canada's trade law, given the degree to which U.S. agriculture is subsidized. It is interesting to note that those commodity groups in Canadian agiculture that have had first-hand experience of U.S. contingent protection practices are confident that the provision in the FTA of mechanisms for the impartial adjudication of trade disputes is superior to both the status quo and the situation threatened by future U.S. trade legislation.

A balanced view is that the FTA is advantageous for the Canadian agrifood system. Consumers benefit from all the provisions. The more competitive components of farm production and food processing have acquired much improved, more assured, and preferred access to an enormous and wealthy market. The least competitive production sectors have retained the bulk of the protection they now enjoy. Disadvantaged groups are few, and the most damaged (grapes and wine) could readily be compensated or assisted to adjust. The Canadian agricultural and food-processing industries will be larger and its participants more prosperous as a result of the inclusion of agriculture in the FTA.

The major lament should be that in the FTA Canada was unable to reduce the subsidies that tilt the competitive playing field in favor of U.S. farmers and food manufacturers, and thereby provide more scope for the release of the Canadian agrifood system's comparative advantage and competitiveness. Additionally, some observers regret that Canadian authorities failed to use the opportunity to shed more of the domestic regulations that burden Canadian consumers, and that prevent the Canadian agrifood system from reaching its full potential.

CHAPTER 6

The Auto Pact: Plus or Minus?

Since 1965 the Canada-U.S. auto pact has been a centrepiece of Canadian commercial policy. By providing duty-free access to the U.S. market for most Canadian automotive products, the pact has been a major reason for the auto industry's improved efficiency and rising exports. Automotive exports to the United States now make up about 7% of Canadian gross domestic product.

Because of progress under the pact, it is not surprising that some Canadians were eager to keep automobiles off the table during the recent free-trade negotiations. Why tinker with a winning combination? The United States, however, insisted on including the automobile industry, mainly because of growing concerns over certain features of Canadian auto policy.

Inclusion of the auto industry — in particular, the elimination of residual auto tariffs — was also important in meeting the test of the General Agreement on Tariffs and Trade (GATT) Article 24, requiring that a free-trade agreement cover substantially all trade. Not only will remaining auto tariffs be eliminated by the Canada-U.S. Free-Trade Agree-

Paul Wonnacott is Professor of Economics, University of Maryland, College Park, MD. His recent related works include *The United States and Canada: The Quest for Free Trade* (Washington, D.C.: Institute for International Economics, 1987), and *U.S. and Canadian Auto Policies in a Changing World Environment* (Toronto: C.D. Howe Institute, 1987).

ment (FTA), but also the FTA includes a major chapter on auto products.

The auto clauses have been attacked by a number of prominent critics, including Premier David Peterson of Ontario and President Bob White of the Canadian Auto Workers. When Canada's trade negotiator Simon Reisman announced that he had negotiated an "auto pact plus," Mr. White was ready with a sharp rejoinder: the Canadian negotiators had settled for an "auto pact minus."

Actually, the FTA strengthens the auto pact in some ways and weakens it in others. A case can be made for either Mr. Reisman's or Mr. White's conclusion. However, determining which is closer to the truth is not the main point. The main point is that the existing situation had become unstable. If the problems in the auto industry had not been dealt with in the recent free-trade negotiations, they would not have simply gone away. Because of these problems, a major confrontation was looming between the two countries. By reducing the potential conflicts, the FTA has made Canadian access to the U.S. market more predictable and secure. And this, after all, was the main reason why Canada initiated the free-trade talks in the first place.

Specifically, the sources of strain under the auto pact have been

- a long-lasting disagreement over Canadian safeguards that accompanied the auto pact. In order to qualify for the right to import automotive products duty-free under the pact, Canadian auto firms have to meet production targets. In simple terms, they have to produce approximately as many cars in Canada as they sell in Canada, and achieve a Canadian value-added in excess of 60% of the value of cars sold in Canada. Firms meeting the safeguards can import duty-free from any country, not just the United States. The safeguards meant that Canada maintained a degree of protection under the auto pact.

- Canadian moves to extend the safeguards to overseas

automobile producers selling in Canada

- competition for overseas plants, including
  - incentives provided in both countries, aimed at attracting new plants
  - Canadian duty-remission programs
  - U.S. foreign-trade zones.

The FTA eliminates or reduces each of these three sources of strain. Although the Canadian safeguards remain, their coverage has been limited. Canada has agreed not to extend pact status to any new members, in contrast to the previous policy of moving toward a requirement that all significant sellers of automobiles in Canada become members. Canada has agreed to eliminate export-based, duty-remission programs at the beginning of 1989 and production-based duty remissions by the end of 1995. Finally, disagreements over U.S. foreign-trade zones are dealt with as part of the general drawback issue.

The major purpose of this chapter will be to look in detail at three major sources of conflict and the ways in which they were handled under the FTA:

- the Canadian export-based duty-remission program
- the Canadian move toward requiring overseas firms to participate in the auto pact, under which they would receive duty-free treatment as a reward for meeting the production levels specified in the safeguards
- the Canadian safeguards themselves

Export-Based Duty Remissions

Under the duty-remission program, Japanese and other overseas producers operating in Canada have an incentive to export from Canada; they are rewarded in the form of a rebate or waiver of duties on imports. For example, a Japanese firm can get back the duty paid on imports of cars from Japan by exporting automotive parts to the United States or elsewhere. This program creates three problems.

- It represents a rather clear subsidy to exports. For example, a Japanese firm may receive a reward of up to $9.20 in duties remitted for every $100 in parts exported; the $9.20 is in effect a subsidy to the export and thus creates problems both under U.S. law and under the GATT Subsidies Code. In this regard, it is important to recognize the distinction between a duty remission and a duty drawback. A duty drawback, which is legal under the GATT, involves the refund of a duty paid on a product when that same product is re-exported. The Canadian duty remissions provide a rebate when a quite different item is exported; the exported item might have been produced 100% in Canada. In recent years some allegations of subsidy have raised complex questions, with unclear answers. It is quite understandable, for example, that Canadians feel that the U.S. government arbitrarily broadened the definition of subsidies in the softwood-lumber case. But there is little doubt that an export-based duty remission constitutes an export subsidy (although the Canadian government does not admit this).

- The duty-remission program has raised the old question associated with the Canadian refusal to phase out the safeguards: Is Canada acting in good faith? One of the things that the United States got out of the auto pact of 1965 was the termination of the old duty-remission program of 1962–63. Indeed, the problems associated with that program had been the precipitating cause of the negotiations that led to the auto pact. A U.S. radiator manufacturer had sued to force the U.S. Treasury to impose a countervailing duty (CVD), as required by U.S. law. Most observers thought the manufacturer would win. To prevent a trade conflict, the auto pact was hurriedly negotiated.

The recent history of duty remissions has not been reassuring to the United States. When Canada introduced a duty-remission program for Volkswagen in 1978, the United States objected. Canada seemed to understand these objections: when duty-remission programs were offered to Japanese firms in 1980, remissions were to be granted only as a reward for exports to countries other than the United States. But in 1984 the U.S. exclusion was dropped.

- The current duty-remission program is more objectionable to the United States than was the old program of 1962–63. The old program was associated with *two-way* trade between Canada and the United States; an export subsidy was provided when firms earned the remission of duties paid on Canadian *imports from the United States*. Under the current remissions, Japanese firms operating in Canada can use *exports to the United States* (which are duty-free under the auto pact) as a way of earning the remission of duties on *imports from Japan*. In other words, the current duty-remission program tends to attract more imports from Japan and push subsidized exports to the United States.

To date, export-based duty remissions have not been very large; they have mainly benefited European firms operating in Canada. However, with the expected large rise in production by Japanese firms in Canada, the duty-remission program might have become significant in dollar terms, as well as symbolically. With the elimination of the export-based duty remissions at the beginning of 1989, this source of conflict will be removed. If nothing had been done it is likely that there would have been a U.S. CVD action against the remissions.

Overseas Producers: Should They Qualify for the Pact?

In the FTA Canada also agreed to limit the pact's membership to current participants, thus reversing the move toward requiring all firms selling significant numbers of automobiles in Canada to meet the safeguards. A set of production-based, duty-remission agreements between the Canadian government and Japanese auto firms was apparently intended as a transitional step toward a full meeting of the safeguards, with the related duty-free privileges.

Participation in the pact by overseas firms raises some of the same issues as the export-based, duty-remission program, although in a more complicated way. To highlight the similarity: if a Japanese auto firm were to achieve pact membership by meeting Canadian production targets, then it would not have to pay duties on its imports from Japan. But, of course, to meet the production targets, it would be encouraged to export from Canada. The most obvious place to send exports would be to the duty-free U.S. market. Again, as in the case of the export-based duty remissions, Canada would be using the carrot of duty-free imports from Japan as a way of pushing exports into the duty-free U.S. market.

The economic and political reasons for Canada wanting to keep the pact open to non-American participants are relatively straightforward. Most obviously, additional overseas trade can provide diversification and a balance to the overwhelming U.S. presence. But the reasons why the United States should object to an arrangement that attracts imports in from Japan and pushes exports out to the United States are also easy to understand. From the U.S. side, an obvious question arises: if Canadians and Japanese want an arrangement for duty-free imports into Canada, to be balanced with exports from Canada, then maybe Japan, not the United States, should take the Canadian exports. Or, to put it another way: if Canada and Japan want to arrange an auto pact of their own, with duty-free exports in *both* directions, that would be one thing. But it is unreasonable for Japan to free-load on the U.S.-Canada pact, exporting duty-free to Canada and expecting the United States to absorb the duty-free exports of Canadian-based Japanese firms. In addition, Japan maintains tariff and other barriers to a flow of auto products from Canada back to Japan.

From the U.S. side, one way out of the problem would have been to request that Canada bilateralize the auto pact. Under the pact, the United States provides preferential duty-free entry to Canadian products; it would not be unreasonable to expect Canada in return to provide preferential duty-free entry only to U.S. products. But such a bilateralization would create problems for U.S. auto firms operating in Canada. Although the overwhelming majority of their imports into Canada come from the United States, these firms also benefit from duty-free imports from overseas. They are now importing about $3 billion Canadian yearly from such non-U.S. sources. With the Canadian tariff on autos and parts at 9.2%, this means that they save about $300 million Canadian annually from the multilateral provisions on the Canadian side of the auto pact. In the summer of 1987 when the U.S. government was considering whether to request that Canada bilateralize the pact, the U.S. Motor Vehicle Manufacturers Association reacted strongly — they were "extremely alarmed."

The outcome of the negotiations was reassuring to current participants in the auto pact: they will continue to enjoy duty-free imports into Canada from any country. But the door has been shut to new participants, and the production-based duty remissions, which represent a halfway station to pact membership, will be terminated by January 1, 1996.

In combination with the end of the export-based duty remissions, these steps mean that the United States will no longer face the prospect of Canadian-based Japanese firms receiving an incentive, in the form of duty remissions or duty waivers, as a reward for exporting to the United States. Of course, if they meet the 50% North American-content rule, the firms will still have duty-free access to the U.S. market; they simply will not receive special incentives for exporting.

This does not mean that Canada is completely out of the

woods. The production-based remissions may still be a source of trouble, as they will remain in force until the end of 1995. One difficulty is that the remission agreements remain secret; without knowing the details, the U.S. Congress is being asked to acquiesce to continuation of the agreements for the next eight years. U.S. government requests for copies of the remission agreements have been rebuffed.

The Canadian Safeguards

With the phasing out of automotive tariffs between Canada and the United States, one of the incentives for auto firms to meet the safeguards will be eliminated. They will no longer face the possibility of huge Canadian duty payments on their imports from the United States if they fail to comply. Consequently, the FTA is sometimes interpreted on both sides of the border as the effective end to the Canadian safeguards. For example, Premier Peterson has spoken of the "elimination of Canadian value-added requirements," while Mr. White has spoken of an auto industry "without safeguards."

However, this is not an accurate conclusion. The Big-Three auto makers still have an incentive to comply — the $300 million Canadian saved annually on duties that would otherwise have to be paid on imports into Canada from overseas sources. Questions may be asked on both sides of the border regarding the safeguards. On the Canadian side the question arises: Have the safeguards been fatally weakened? On the U.S. side the question is the opposite: Did the U.S. negotiators make a mistake in tacitly accepting the continuation of the safeguards and not insisting on their elimination?

First, consider the Canadian question. It is true that an extremely strong incentive to comply with the safeguards was eliminated — namely the threat of huge duty payments on imports from the United States. But the question may at least be asked whether this threat could be carried out in practice. Like an atomic weapon, it may be too powerful and dangerous to use. Before Canada presented auto firms with huge duty bills on imports from the United States, serious thought would presumably have to be given to the possibility of U.S. retaliation. The more modest weapon — duties on imports from overseas — is more usable, both because of its size and because it does not apply to exports from the United States. (Japan would be much less likely to retaliate to the collection of such duties because Japan has no duty-free agreement with Canada, and because Japanese manufacturers operating in Canada will already be paying duties.) A $300-million incentive should be sufficient to ensure compliance in the foreseeable future. This is particularly so because Chrysler, which previously was in the weakest position to comply, now has much more elbow room because of the recent acquisition of American Motors and its up-to-date Canadian facilities.

This leads to the U.S. question: Did not the United States make a mistake in allowing the safeguards to persist under the FTA? The problem, from the U.S. side, is that there is no clear national interest. Quite apart from a possible conflict between the interests of auto producers and those of consumers, there is a conflict between the interests of the Big Three, on the one hand, and the interests of parts producers and the United Auto Workers (UAW) on the other.

The safeguards are inextricably tied up with duty-free imports from third countries into Canada by the Big Three. Without the safeguards, the auto pact would have been bilateralized and the Big Three would have lost their access to duty-free imports from overseas — resulting in a duty payment of $300 million Canadian annually. On the other hand, the UAW and U.S. parts producers *wanted* the auto pact bilateralized and the safeguards eliminated. The safeguards mean that U.S. (and Canadian) parts producers face duty-free competition from overseas firms in getting contracts to supply the Big Three in Canada. The safeguards also prevent U.S. parts producers from competing freely with Canadian producers in the Canadian parts market. Julian Morris, president of the Automotive Parts and Accessories Association, has criticized the FTA as "unfair" because it "fails to eliminate Canadian protection of its auto/auto-parts sectors. It would subject one-third of bilateral trade to a pro-Canadian managed, not free, trade regime."

In short, there is a conflict of views within the United States. The recent FTA negotiations made the United States address the question specifically: Did it really want an elimination of the safeguards and the straight bilateralization of the auto pact that this would have involved? The answer, apparently, was "No."

Finally, it is interesting to observe an apparent paradox in the positions taken by the labor unions on the two sides of the border. Both the U.S. and the Canadian auto workers' unions are critical of the FTA. Yet the FTA moves at least one step toward a reduction in automotive imports from overseas: the Canadian duty-remission schemes are to end, and no new entrants into the auto pact are to be permitted. As the FTA will thus work toward an increase in overall North American automotive production, it would seem that at least one of the unions, and perhaps both, should welcome the FTA — yet they are both opposed. One explanation apparently is that neither side got everything it wanted. The Canadian union wanted no change in Canadian automotive policies; the U.S. union wanted a complete dismantling of the special incentives to produce in Canada. What they got was a compromise — a not uncommon occurrence in international negotiations.

Conclusions

My overall conclusion is that the automotive clauses in the FTA are about as good as could be expected. The negotiators picked their way through a complex set of issues, resulting in elimination of duty remissions, and partial bilateralization of the auto pact from the Canadian side, by limiting its privileges to present members.

It is hard to imagine a substantially better outcome, under the circumstances. It is true that the auto clauses of the FTA are a bit untidy, but it should be recognized that these clauses grew out of the same dynamic process as the auto pact itself: unilateral Canadian action to deal with a situation that Canada considered unsatisfactory; the threat of CVD action by the United States; and an international agreement to avoid an explosion.

My responses to some of the specific questions raised in the Introduction of this book are as follows.

- What did Canada gain? The answer is, a great reduction in the risk of a CVD action in the automotive sector. The FTA resulted in U.S. acceptance of the safeguards, at least tacitly.

- What did Canada not gain? It did not gain blanket U.S. approval to engage in duty-remission schemes without limit and without the risk of CVD action. (It is not clear that Canada really hoped to achieve such a goal, but there was no prospect that the United States would grant it.)

- What did Canada give up? The FTA reversed the move toward required pact membership for all sellers of cars in Canada. (It is not clear that such required membership would have been in Canada's interest — but that is a topic for another publication.)

- What did Canada not give up? It did not give up the central features of the auto pact, including the safeguards and duty-free access to the U.S. market.

Finally, what would the consequences be if the FTA were rejected? For the auto industry, a rejection of the FTA would leave unfinished business on the table. The pre-existing situation is quite unstable, particularly with the Canadian duty-remission programs. There would be two possible outcomes. Specific negotiations could be undertaken to deal with the outstanding problems. In this case, something like the auto clauses of the FTA would represent about as good an outcome as can be envisaged. The other alternative would be to do nothing. But this would risk a major confrontation within the next few years over Canadian subsidies on automotive exports to the United States.

We can address our auto problems now or we can address them later, when they have become much more intractable. Fortunately, the problems were addressed in the recent free-trade negotiations.

CHAPTER 7
Energy

The energy chapter of the Canada-U.S. Free-Trade Agreement (FTA) has created more ill-informed hysteria than almost any other part of the agreement. Opponents of the trade deal reacted instantly in October 1987 to the preliminary elements of the agreement on energy with a host of dire predictions, including:

> *U.S.-controlled companies will drain Canada's reserves to supply the United States.*
> – Mel Hurtig, Council of Canadians

> *Ottawa has surrendered its capacity to regulate exports of energy to the advantage of the Canadian national interest and consumers.*
> – Premier Joseph Ghiz, Prince Edward Island

> *The free trade agreement results in a continental energy policy which would force Canada to share energy shortages with the United States and would prevent it from using its energy resources for industrial advantage or to protect consumers from future price shocks.*
> – David Crane, *The Toronto Star*

The FTA energy chapter seemed to come as a surprise to

Edward A. Carmichael is Vice-President and Director of Policy Research, C.D. Howe Institute, Toronto. His related publications include *Canada's Energy Policy: 1988 and Beyond* (editor) (Toronto: C.D. Howe Institute, 1984): *New Stresses on Confederation* (Toronto: C.D. Howe Institute, 1986); and *Tackling the Federal Deficit* (Toronto: C.D. Howe Institute, 1984).

both advocates and opponents of free trade. There was an initial impression that the United States had won a major concession from Canada that went well beyond commitments in other areas of the FTA. Although Canada's energy minister, Marcel Masse, and chief trade negotiator, Simon Reisman, issued statements contradicting the fears, it was not until the legal language of the FTA was made available on December 10, 1987, that it was possible to say categorically that fears that U.S. interests, rather than Canadian government policies, would determine the future development and use of Canadian energy were totally mistaken.

What has become clear based on accurate interpretations of the FTA energy chapter is that not only have the fears been greatly exaggerated, but also the real benefits to Canada of the agreement have been understated. The energy agreement does *not* mean that

- Canada loses control over the development and use of its energy: provincial governments and the National Energy Board retain their ability to regulate exploration, production, and prices

- U.S.-owned companies can buy up Canadian energy reserves: Canada's policy preventing takeovers of financially healthy Canadian energy companies was grandfathered

- Canada cannot cushion the blow of a future sharp increase in energy prices: Canada can maintain oil prices below world levels although this would have to apply also to exports to the United States; alternatively, Canada could use personal transfers such as an energy tax credit to cushion the impact on consumers

- Canada will be unable to use its energy resources for industrial advantage: Canada will continue to benefit industrially from its abundant and secure supplies of energy

What the FTA *does* is to

- prohibit government intervention to set prices that discriminate against U.S. purchasers

- prohibit export taxes

- prohibit most restrictions on energy exports and imports except where these are permitted under the General Agreement on Tariffs and Trade (GATT) due to short supply, conservation, or national security

- establish rights of consultation in cases where regulatory actions distort trade

Perhaps the most important thing to understand about the energy chapter of the Canada-U.S. FTA is that it represents nothing more than an extension and clarification of Canada's existing rights and obligations under the GATT. The proportional sharing commitment to which many critics have objected, for example, is not new. It is merely a reaffirmation of what Canada and the United States have already agreed to as members of the GATT. Therefore, those who criticize the FTA on the grounds that Canada could have obtained a better deal through multilateral negotiations are entirely wrong in relation to the energy chapter. Indeed, based on their rhetorical comments, it appears that some critics of the energy chapter would oppose Canada living up to its existing GATT commitments on trade in energy.

The FTA Energy Chapter

The section of the FTA dealing with energy, like most parts of the agreement, closely parallels the GATT rules. Energy is dealt with in chapter 9 of the FTA, which contains nine Articles and two annexes.

Article 901 indicates the coverage of energy products as defined under the harmonized system by which imports are classified. The only wrinkle is that electricity, the status of which has been unclear under the GATT, is clearly included in the FTA. Since U.S. coal interests have been threatening protectionist actions against Canadian electricity, its inclusion is a clear benefit to Canada.

Article 902 reaffirms both countries' GATT rights and obligations. This is very important, both because it clearly underscores that these commitments are not new and because it clearly prohibits restrictions on energy trade, with a few important existing GATT exceptions permitted. Restrictions on exports will be allowed during periods of short supply, conservation of an exhaustible resource, national security, or imposition of price controls but these are subject to certain limitations set out in Article 904.

Article 903 states both countries' agreement not to impose any type of export tax or duty on energy. Imposing an export tax — the most straightforward method of discriminating against foreign purchasers — is inconsistent with free trade.

Article 904 reaffirms both countries' rights to restrict exports for the reasons stated in Article 902, as long as the country imposing the restriction provides "proportional access" to the other partner as required under GATT Article XX. This is the "proportional access" that some initially saw as an Achilles heel of the FTA. On closer examination, it turns out to be a sharing principle that Canada, along with 101 other countries, is already committed to under the GATT.

What does "proportional access" mean? First, as long as markets continue to function freely so that demand and supply remain relatively balanced, the proportional-access rule would have no effect. This is because it is only applied if the exporting country (Canada) decides that it wants to impose export controls. Canada could decide, for example, that because its reserves of, say, crude oil were diminishing, it wanted to restrict production. Canada could then restrict exports to the United States, but only in the same proportion that it restricted total production. The exact amount would be equal to the average proportion of Canadian crude oil that the United States had purchased over the previous thirty-six months. This specific formula actually clarifies and tightens up the meaning of proportional access, which is relatively vague under the GATT rules.

Proportional access is not threatening when one understands that

- it is Canada that determines if and when such sharing will be invoked

- Canada is under no obligation to sell any particular quantity to the United States as long as it provides U.S. buyers with access to the required proportion of Canadian supply at commercial terms

- Canadians can continue to compete commercially to buy any amount of Canadian energy supply up to the total amount

Article 905 provides both countries with the right to formal consultation over any changes in regulatory policies that distort energy trade. The U.S. Federal Energy Regulatory Commission (FERC) has recently taken decisions that discriminate against Canadian natural gas. Although these decisions will not be rolled back, in the event of any future regulatory actions Canada could require consultations at the Cabinet level, between energy ministers, to resolve the dispute. This is a much stronger position than Canada has had in past disputes.

Article 906 recognizes the importance of oil and gas fiscal incentives for maintaining reserves levels. This does not constitute an exemption from countervailing duties but it does provide both countries with some leeway in encouraging exploration and development.

Article 907 defines "national security" for the purpose of the FTA more precisely than it is defined under the GATT. This is a benefit to Canada since, in the case of energy, national security is often the battle cry of U.S. energy producers when they face competitive imports. Under the tighter definition, the United States would only be able to invoke national security to restrict Canadian exports to the United States if it faced a military threat.

Article 908 says the FTA is not inconsistent with the International Energy Agreement (IEA) and that IEA commitments supersede those contained in the FTA. This is an important assurance to other IEA members that Canada and the United States will live up to their international commitments on energy, including the oil-sharing arrangement under the IEA, which is considerably more onerous than the proportional-sharing arrangement in the FTA.

Article 909 contains definitions of some key words and phrases in the chapter.

The chapter also contains important appendices that

- exempt Canada from the prohibition on exports of Alaskan oil, up to 50 000 barrels per day

- eliminate U.S. restrictions on enrichment of Canadian uranium

- exempt the United States from Canada's requirement that Canadian uranium be upgraded before it is exported

- require the U.S. Bonneville Power Administration to afford British Columbia Hydro fair access to its distribution lines.

That is what is in the FTA. It is straightforward and clear. It does not create some new continental energy policy. Rather, it confirms and strengthens the existing free-trade environment enjoyed by the energy sector, while reaffirming and clarifying both countries' rights and obligations under the GATT and IEA rules.

Benefits of the FTA for Canada

Just as fears about free trade in energy have been overstated, benefits of free trade in energy have not been fully understood. The major benefits of free trade in energy are likely to be gained in the longer term, after the year 2000.

The short-term benefits are small because something very close to free trade in energy has existed between Canada and the United States since 1985, when the Canadian government dropped the creaking system of regulated oil and natural gas prices introduced as part of the National Energy Program of 1980. There have been no tariffs on the main energy products, with the exception of small U.S. tariffs on crude oil and petroleum products. Because much of the bilateral energy trade is already "free" the short-term benefits will be small.

There is an important difference, however, between a temporary, voluntary period of free trade as has existed for the past three years, and a bilateral treaty locking free trade in energy into a much larger agreement. A treaty will provide stability and confidence that free trade in energy will last. Investors can then make their decisions based on the knowledge that the rules will not change. They will also know that large, high-cost projects that only make economic sense if a large market exists are now more viable. This is a real plus, after the experience of the 1970s, when Canadian taxpayers spent billions bankrolling Petro-Canada and others to look for energy in the Arctic and Atlantic frontiers, only to learn that the cost of producing and transporting the energy discovered would be economically viable only if the volume of energy produced was extremely large. Under these circumstances, the value of a large, secure market to underwrite the cost and risk should be readily apparent.

Confidence in a stable energy policy and the availability of a large secure market should mean increased activity in the Canadian energy sector over the longer term. But what about individual sectors?

Uranium: Canada's uranium industry is a big winner under free trade. Canada is the world's largest exporter of uranium. Mines in northern Saskatchewan are high grade and highly competitive internationally. The U.S. industry, on the other hand, is in relative decline, mining much lower-grade ore bodies that have become relatively high cost. Under these circumstances, U.S. uranium producers have used both political action and legal proceedings to try to restrict enrichment of foreign uranium. A case currently before the U.S. Supreme Court could result in a total embargo on all imported uranium in the United States. If this occurred, Canada would lose a market of $400 million, with most of the impact being felt in northern Saskatchewan.

With the FTA, Canadian uranium will be exempt from any import restrictions. In the short term, an important market will be maintained; in the longer term, the development potential for the Canadian uranium industry will be greatly expanded.

Crude Oil and Natural Gas: The most important benefit of free trade to Canada's oil and gas industry is the protection it provides against foolish Canadian energy policies. The battles of the 1970s and early 1980s between the federal government and the producing provinces over prices, royalties, taxes, and export restrictions greatly damaged activity and confidence levels in the industry. With the FTA in place, government intervention to regulate prices will be much less attractive. Export controls, export taxes, and minimum export prices will be ruled out. This means that Canadian governments will not be able to intervene to set export prices above domestic energy prices as the federal government did after 1973 and in the National Energy Program of 1980. Canada's policies during this period violated the GATT rules and strained Canada-U.S. energy relations. Domestically, it was eventually recognized that the two-price policy was inefficient as well as regionally divisive. Thus, entering into an agreement that commits Canada not to repeat its past energy policy mistakes must be seen as a major positive for Canada's oil and gas industry.

There will be some small, immediate benefits to the oil

industry from the reduction in U.S. crude-oil and products tariffs. In the longer run, however, the main benefit to the oil and gas industry will be the ability to attract capital to develop large-scale projects in remote frontier areas and pipelines to bring the energy to markets in Canada and the United States.

Electricity: Trade in electricity has always been free of tariffs. As Canadian exports increased substantially in volume after the mid-1970s, however, threats of U.S. protectionism have increased. The inclusion of electricity in the FTA therefore comes at an important time, when the industry is entering a phase in which its future rate of growth will depend significantly on secure access to the U.S. market.

Canada's net exports of electricity to the United States in 1986 were valued at approximately $1 billion, with the majority in the form of short-term or "interruptible" contracts. As Hydro-Québec's recent sale to New England demonstrates, however, future sales will increasingly be long-term contracts that require new generating capacity. Manitoba and B.C. Hydro also are following this strategy. Therefore, the ability of Canadian electrical utilities to meet the terms of their long-term contracts will be enhanced by free trade and this will encourage U.S. utilities to consider imports from Canada.

One confusion that has arisen is that, under free trade, Canada would have to sell electricity to the United States at the same price as it is sold in Canada. The confusion arises from a misunderstanding of how electricity is priced. Electricity is sold under contracts with a wide range of terms and conditions and at a wide range of prices. Guaranteed, long-term electricity such as that now being sold to the United States carries a higher price than short-term, interruptible electricity.

What can be said about electricity pricing under free trade is that it will continue at commercial levels agreed to by the buyers and sellers. Where commercial terms differ, prices for electricity sold in Canada or the United States will also differ.

These prices will still be subject to regulatory tests such as the National Energy Board's tests that the price be sufficient to recover all costs and that it be no less than the price available to Canadians for equivalent service in the same area.

As is true for other segments of the energy industry, then, the main benefits to Canada of free trade in electricity will arise in the longer term, as Canada is increasingly seen by U.S. consumers as a dependable, competitive supplier.

Energy Policy: Flexibility and Security

Even after the facts about free trade in energy became clear, opponents of the FTA continued to assert that Canada's ability to maintain an independent energy policy had been greatly reduced. In one sense, this is true. Canada agreed not to take some mutually harmful actions against the United States (such as the export taxes and discriminatory prices it adopted in the 1970s) in return for U.S. agreement not to take mutually harmful actions against Canada (such as regulatory actions to block Canadian imports of uranium, electricity, and natural gas). But ruling out mutually harmful actions does nothing to reduce Canada's ability to adopt beneficial, independent energy policies.

Canada retains its ability to

- control the pace of development and production of its energy resources

- prohibit takeovers of financially healthy oil and gas companies

- use fiscal incentives to encourage exploration and development

- regulate prices or to use the national tax and transfer systems to cushion the impact of any future sharp energy-price increase

Canada need not consult with the United States nor harmonize its policies with those of the United States in any of these areas. Therefore, each of the dire predictions turns out to be wrong.

Canada's energy security and that of the United States should be enhanced by free trade. Canada's vast frontier potential is unlikely to be developed to supply the Canadian market alone. For frontier megaprojects to be economically viable, very large volumes of production are required. Undeveloped, these frontier reserves contribute nothing to Canada's security. If free trade helps to bring this energy to market, it will enhance the energy security of both countries.

Conclusions

Free trade in energy has been a fact since 1985. The benefits have already begun to show. Yet the free trade that currently exists cannot be seen as secure, particularly given the wild swings in energy policy of the last fifteen years. The full benefits of free trade in energy can be achieved if secured within a long-term treaty of the type provided by the Canada-U.S. FTA.

CHAPTER 8
Foreign Direct Investment

What will Canada gain and give up with regard to foreign direct investment by the terms of the Canada-U.S. Free-Trade Agreement (FTA)? To answer this question, two issues must be considered. First, how does the FTA affect the power to regulate such investment? Second, how will the reduction of trade barriers affect the flows of such investment? It is my feeling that not much change in present regulation is involved. If Canadians want to take a stronger line in the future with such investment, however, they will have to look to other instruments. Meanwhile, Canada's multinationals have secured greater access to the U.S. market in both trade and investment. Contrary to many predictions, I believe that substantial divestment by foreign multinationals in Canada is unlikely. To the contrary, there is likely to be increased direct investment in both directions for a some time.

Broadly, the provisions on foreign direct investment are as follows:

A.E. Safarian is Professor of Economics, University of Toronto. Supporting references for the points made in this chapter can be found in articles he has published in D.W. Conklin and T.J. Courchene (eds.), *Canadian Trade at a Crossroads: Options for New International Agreements* (Ontario Economic Council, 1985), and M.G. Smith and F. Stone (eds.), *Assessing the Canada-U.S. Free Trade Agreement* (Ottawa: Institute for Research on Public Policy, 1987).

- National treatment will be provided for each other's investors. "National treatment" means that, with certain exceptions, foreign-controlled firms are treated no less favorably than domestically controlled firms in similar situations. More particularly, each party agrees that it will not require that minimum levels of equity be held by nationals, that it will avoid export or import requirements when it regulates foreign investment, and that it will act fairly when expropriating. Otherwise, national treatment allows each country to regulate as it chooses, as long as the regulations are applied evenly to each other's firms.

- However, all existing laws, regulations, and published policies and practices not in conformity with these obligations can be retained. That includes a long list in each country.

- Canada agrees to progressively raise the exemption level for review of U.S. acquisitions of Canadian-owned firms from $5 million in gross assets to $150 million in constant dollars. Review of indirect acquisitions (i.e., those where the parent firm's ownership changes) will be phased out.

- The cultural industries are generally excluded from the FTA but each country reserves the right to take action under its trade laws, as at present, should policies be undertaken that damage its interests. Present policies reducing foreign ownership in petroleum, natural gas, and uranium will also continue: the higher levels noted in the preceding point will not apply here either.

- Canada agrees to give U.S. firms national treatment in relation to ownership of Canadian financial institutions. This involves a significant change from present Canadian policies. The United States agrees to reciprocate in some aspects of national treatment if and when it succeeds in passing relevant legislation. There is also agreement to cover a number of other services sectors. These points are dealt with further in chapter 4, "Services," in this book.

The FTA will not change much of what the two countries are now doing in terms of regulating such investment. The exemption given present laws and policies generally means that sectors already closed to foreign investment stay that way. One notable exception is in financial services, where the balance of concessions favors the U.S. side. Canada also made concessions in terms of review of inward direct investment, because the United States has no comparable review process.

Little has been given up in terms of Canada's actual review practices, however. Investment Canada does not review new investments, nor has it rejected any of the acquisitions it has handled to date. The Foreign Investment Review Agency operated almost as liberally in its last two years. About two-thirds of total Canadian-controlled assets will still be reviewable when the new threshold on direct acquisitions is in effect, using all the present criteria except stock equity and trade performance. Review of indirect acquisitions has been used to some effect in the petroleum and cultural industries, where the existing provisions are retained.

The United States, in turn, has given up the right to apply a review process against Canadian multinationals, in the event that such a process is introduced against other countries. That is not a remote possibility, given the substantial and growing foreign takeover of U.S. industry. Therefore, one can consider the FTA as guaranteeing access to the U.S. market by Canadian multinationals, which have become important investors there, while allowing Canada to continue to review larger acquisitions by U.S.-controlled firms. The importance of such investment access will become more evident later in this chapter when it is noted that such investment is most often a vehicle for increasing trade.

The relatively liberal Canadian approach to inward direct investment in recent years, and the strenuous efforts to attract it, are part of a worldwide trend in the face of slow growth or high unemployment. Canada also has some special reasons for moving away from a policy based on trying to negotiate more benefit from multinationals to one based on attempts to make Canada a more attractive setting for multinational activity, both foreign and domestic. Foreign control of Canadian industry, which some have dreaded for a variety of reasons, has fallen steadily from about 36% in 1970 to about 26% today. Multinationals have concentrated their newer investments in relatively few markets, and Canadian authorities have been working hard to capture more of that investment. Finally, Canada's multinationals have come of age very quickly. In 1974 Canada's stock of direct investment abroad as a percentage of the foreign-owned stock in Canada was 20%, while today it is at least 60% and rising rapidly.

One result has been to lead the Canadian authorities to emphasize some of the concerns of an important *home* country for multinationals, particularly the need for a stable and non-restrictive investment environment for such firms. In addition, while there are several good reasons why Canadian firms invest in the United States, the Canadian government hopes that the FTA will slow those investments abroad that are the result of U.S. protectionist trade policies.

Some *potentially* significant concessions were made by Canada. For example, excluding the exceptions already noted, in future Canada will not be able to review new inward direct investment or foreign acquisitions of the large number of smaller firms with assets below $150 million. What one concludes about these concessions depends on what one thought of the particular policies used in the first place. If you believe that they were fundamentally in error — largely wrong about their assumptions regarding the effects of multinationals, and counter-productive in practice — then you will suffer no great pang of regret over the fact that history cannot be repeated in quite this way.

What if one believes that there are some valid concerns about multinationals, however, or if a different economic environment or other circumstances raise strong calls for intervention? In such circumstances what the FTA does is to require that governments find ways to deal with the issues that do not discriminate by nationality of ownership. The outcome should be to lead governments to look more closely at the underlying sources or extent of the problems, rather than simply to concentrate on the multinational firm, and to apply remedies to all firms that qualify, wherever owned. The discipline imposed by this could be salutary, or at least no worse than what happens now.

More specifically, Canada has retained the power to review larger acquisitions on a reduced set of criteria. In the Competition Act of 1986 Canada also has what may turn out to be an effective set of civil law proceedings to deal with mergers and monopolies (now called "abuse of dominant position") that substantially lessen competition. Experience elsewhere, including in the United States, suggests that such powers can be used effectively to discipline international mergers, at least with regard to a wide range of anti-competitive practices.

In addition, Canada has the power to use a variety of across-the-board fiscal policies that will impact substantially on investment, as long as these policies do not discriminate by nationality of ownership. Indeed, the two countries reserved the right to apply new taxes and subsidies that do not involve "arbitrary or unjustifiable discrimination" by nationality of investor. While hedged by the dispute-settlement mechanism, this allows more leeway than across-the-board measures. Contrary to what some fear, Canada retains more or less its present powers to engage in a considerable range of industrial policies, subject only to the investment and trade provisions of the FTA. Of course, if such policies are trade-distorting they will be subject to U.S. trade law, but they are subject to such law and the related procedures now. Only a strong code on subsidies binding *both* parties would have changed this and such a code was not negotiated — or at least not yet.

Therefore, it would appear that Canada did not give up much in terms of present policy practices. Canada did concede what are potentially significant review powers with regard to the future, but retains a considerable range of over-all and industrial policies related to investment.

What will the FTA mean in terms of the flows of direct investment? Many Canadians appear to have a love/hate relationship with multinationals. They want to regulate them to avoid certain problems or secure certain benefits, but they also do not want them to leave, or at least not in ways that cause any dislocation. One major concern is that, in the absence of protection, a great many foreign-owned firms will close their plants here and supply the Canadian market from the United States. Moreover, it is said that efforts to attract new direct investment here are doomed to fail when one cannot block import penetration of the market. A report for the Government of Ontario has argued in these terms, as have some who are concerned about the employment record of existing foreign-owned firms.

There is no doubt that some existing foreign-controlled subsidiaries will close down with a free-trade agreement, as will some Canadian-owned plants. Other firms that might have established in Canada because of tariffs will not do so. But the size of these divestments is not likely to be as large or unmanageable as some have suggested, and there are offset-ting increases in investment that should exceed these decreases by a considerable margin. There are at least four reasons to doubt the pessimistic scenario.

First, multinationals favor subsidiaries in many activities, rather than exports or licences, simply because subsidiaries give increased profits. They do so, for example, by slowing the loss of information to competitors and by reducing the costs of transferring technology. The tariff-factory argument suggests direct investment substitutes for imports, while the global experience of foreign trade and direct investment ris-ing together suggests that they are largely complementary.

Second, having decided to use a subsidiary, the investors will consider in which country to locate on the basis of four broad factors: the size and growth of markets, costs of pro-duction and distribution, the nature of the competition they face, and the attitudes of government to business as expressed in a variety of fiscal and regulatory policies. There is evidence that protective barriers can affect the location of investment, but the statistical studies suggest that the other variables just noted matter far more in the typical case.

A third point concerns the fate of the large number of existing subsidiaries under a free-trade regime. It is well known that many of these have unit costs in excess of plants in the United States. There is concern, therefore, that the parent firm's strategy would dictate closure or reduction of the Canadian subsidiary. No doubt that will happen in some cases. However, what must be remembered is that a bilateral free-trade area changes all four of the major investment determinants just noted, and does so in ways that are largely favorable to Canada. The expanded and more assured access to the U.S. market, combined with the spur of increased import competition, give substantial incentives to manufacturers to drop some lines and to specialize more fully in others. More efficient scale and lower unit costs are the typical outcome. The major published studies of what would happen in Canada with free trade are almost all favorable in this respect. These studies generally conclude that Canada would be a competitive source for a wide range of manufactures, and that the *overall* effects on income, investment, and employment are positive.

A major reason for the outcomes just noted is that the rationalization of production occurs mainly within firms and industries rather than between them, thus minimizing the adjustments involved for labor, capital, and communities. I do not want to minimize the fact of downward adjustments of employment in some industries or to diminish in any way the need to assure that programs are available to deal with this. However, experience in other trading areas and in Canada supports the view taken here about the nature of the adjustment process. During the 1970s the combination of pressure from falling tariffs, increasing sources of international competition, and the oil-price shocks forced adjustments on Canadian industry that were much larger than those to be expected from a bilateral free-trade arrangement that is phased in gradually. Studies for the Economic Council of Canada show that both increased import *and* export penetration occurred in a wide range of manufactures, even excluding automobiles and parts. This pattern of adjustment occurred in both foreign-owned and domestically owned firms, although it went further in the latter, which started from a less efficient base.

Finally, if one looks at the competitive process by which firms adjust to free trade, even more doubts are raised about the view that foreign direct investment will be reduced. Firms are not in a position to export to a foreign market just because government barriers to trade have been eliminated or stabilized, even if transport costs are low enough to allow trade. There are established competitors in the other market that will attempt to protect their market shares by a wide variety of tactics designed to prevent entry. The potential entrant may decide, therefore, that a less disturbing or more effective way to expand would be through acquiring an existing firm rather than through direct exports, or to enter into a licensing arrangement or joint venture with a foreign firm. Of course, these and other tactics are also open to the foreign firm as it contemplates entry to the Canadian market.

What these possibilities have in common is *increased* foreign direct investment and technology contacts in both directions. These techniques also typically involve a significant amount of exchange of goods and services between the related parties. Again it must be pointed out that it is a mistake to think of trade and foreign direct investment simply or mainly as substitutes for each other. Research has shown, for example, that investments by overseas and European multinationals grew rapidly in the European Economic Community as internal tariffs came down and foreign trade increased.

Turning from manufacturing to natural resources, free trade is likely to lead to an increased investment in Canada by both foreign and Canadian multinationals. Most studies show that Canada already has a comparative advantage in a number of primary resource and primary manufacturing industries, among others. The removal of even small barriers to exports (or the reduced threat of such barriers) could significantly increase investments to process such products further, wherever transport costs allow export. As for the service industries, some, such as banking, prefer subsidiaries or branches rather than trade when they go abroad. Removal of barriers in such industries should increase foreign direct investment.

Finally, many multinationals in third countries would hesitate to produce in Canada today for the combined Canada-U.S. market simply because export access to the larger U.S. market could be blocked. This concern should be reduced or removed with free trade. As already noted, moreover, location decisions by multinationals depend on a large variety of market, cost, competition, and policy variables, many of which change in Canada's favor with freer trade.

Fears of substantial divestment of multinational capital are much exaggerated. There may well be increased investment flows in both directions for a time. The increased investment flows might lead to an increase in foreign ownership of some sectors of Canadian industry in the short term. Over time, however, a more efficient industry, thanks in part to the FTA, should allow more firms to compete and expand without having to seek a buyer, whether domestic or foreign.

What happens if this analysis is wrong and there is a massive divestment of capital from Canada because of freer trade? Several adjustments would limit the damage. The value of the Canadian dollar would fall, increasing the cost of transferring funds out of Canada and making Canada a better location for export. Moreover, such a fire sale of foreign-owned assets would mean low prices for them. This in turn would tempt other investors to try to operate the assets, perhaps in conjunction with a technology or marketing licence negotiated with the original owners. That is a pattern that has been seen repeatedly in recent years as international competition has forced economic restructuring of industry. For reasons noted above, however, Canada is unlikely to experience massive divestment because of free trade.

CHAPTER 9
Dispute Settlement

The dispute-settlement mechanisms of the Canada-U.S. Free-Trade Agreement (FTA) are not perfect. However, they are a significant improvement over the current system for resolving trade disputes between our two countries. They are also markedly better than the dispute-settlement mechanisms of other free-trade area agreements and the General Agreement on Tariffs and Trade (GATT). Most importantly, they represent a break with the pattern of unilateralism that has characterized Canada-U.S. trade relations in the last few years.

In the FTA Canada gained a new set of binational procedures and institutions for avoiding and resolving trade disputes. Two chapters of the FTA are devoted exclusively to dispute settlement: "Institutional Provisions" and "Binational Dispute Settlement in Anti-dumping and Countervailing Duty Cases." The former will establish new formal notification and consultation procedures that should act as an early warning mechanism, to resolve potential problems before they arise or nip them in the bud. Also, a Canada-U.S. Trade Commission will be established that will have the authority to select appropriate methods for resolving particular disputes.

Debra P. Steger practises law with Fraser & Beatty in Ottawa. She specializes in the areas of international trade and competition law and policy, advising clients on the Canada-U.S. trade negotiations, investment, anti-dumping, countervail, mergers, customs and other import/export matters. Ms. Steger is the author of *A Concise Guide to the Canada-United States Free Trade Agreement* (forthcoming from Carswell Legal Publications) as well as several articles on U.S. and Canadian trade laws and the Canada-U.S. trade negotiations.

Where a dispute is not resolved within a short period of time, the commission will be required to appoint either an arbitration panel or a panel of experts to resolve the matter. In many cases, decisions of arbitration panels will be binding on the two governments.

The anti-dumping and countervailing-duty provisions, while not perfect, provide significant advantages over the existing system. The most important accomplishment of the FTA is the serious commitment of Canada and the United States to develop a new system of trade laws, applicable in both countries, over a period of five to seven years. The failure of the negotiators to achieve a new binational system of trade laws has been hailed by many critics as a major reason for not supporting the FTA.

It is indeed unfortunate that the negotiators were not able to agree to abolish the anti-dumping laws or develop a new set of unambiguous, predictable rules concerning subsidies. Regulation of unfair foreign-trade practices has proved to be a complex and fractious subject within the GATT. Considering the deeply held concerns in both Canada and the United States about maintaining sovereignty over important matters of public policy, it is not surprising that the negotiators could not do more in this difficult and sensitive area.

The compromise struck in this vital area is unique. First, the two countries agreed that their primary objective will be to negotiate and implement a new system of trade laws within five to seven years. The penalty for non-compliance is serious: either country can terminate the entire FTA on six months' notice. In the interim, a new, binational-panel system will be established to take the place of judicial review of final anti-dumping and countervailing-duty orders where requested by either country. In addition, the FTA will establish a legislative watchdog to ensure that Canadian and U.S. anti-dumping and countervailing-duty laws are not made more protectionist.

Before the United States amends its trade laws in future, Congress will be required to specifically name Canada in any legislation designed to affect Canadian industries. Also, the United States will be required to provide written notice to the Canadian government and an opportunity for consultation. At present, there is no formal mechanism requiring the two governments to communicate with each other prior to the enactment of new trade legislation. If consultations fail to achieve a consensus solution, Canada may request that a binational panel be formed to consider whether the proposed U.S. legislation is consistent with the GATT and the related anti-dumping and subsidies codes, as well as with the objectives and purposes of the FTA.

There are several advantages to these new binational procedures for anti-dumping and countervailing-duty cases. First, the legislative watchdog should inhibit Congress from changing the U.S. trade laws to make them more protectionist. Second, the binational composition of the panels should enhance the impartiality and objectivity of agency decisions. There is a strongly held perception among Canadians that the 1986 preliminary determination by the Department of Commerce in the softwood-lumber case was influenced by political considerations.

The availability of an impartial, binational body of experts to review agency decisions or controversial legislative amendments should help to reduce perceptions that the U.S. trade laws are being applied in an unfair manner. The binational panels should permit a full airing of different interpretations on difficult legal issues, such as the definition of "countervailable subsidy." If the panels are used with some frequency, their deliberations may assist in achieving a consensus on some of the critical issues to be resolved in the development of a new system of trade laws.

The binational panel system will be faster, simpler, and cheaper than the current system. Timeliness is by far the most important advantage of the binational-panel procedures over the existing system. The binational process would have made a difference in the 1986 softwood-lumber case. In that case the Canadian industry had several arguable issues that were worth pursuing in the courts. However, it might have taken four to five years before the courts would have issued a final decision in the case. The current system is extremely expensive for Canadian exporters. Not only do they have to pay the full expenses of litigation but also, after an affirmative Department of Commerce preliminary determination, duties are payable on any products exported. In the softwood-lumber case the Canadian industry would have had to pay approximately $600 million U.S. per year in preliminary duties while the case was being heard in the courts. The new binational-panel review system will ensure that cases are determined within a maximum of 315 days after a final agency order has been made.

Cost savings also will result for private parties involved in anti-dumping or countervailing-duty cases. Currently, Canadian exporters involved in a U.S. anti-dumping or counter-vailing-duty investigation have to pay the full costs of presenting their case before the Department of Commerce, the International Trade Commission, the Court of International Trade, and other courts, as well as government departments and Congress. A request for review and presentation of a case under the new binational-panel system must be made by a member government. Therefore, the cost to a private firm or firms engaged in a countervailing-duty or anti-dumping case will be reduced.

The FTA also provides for substantive changes to the safe-guards or escape-clause laws of both countries. The shakes-and-shingles and specialty-steel cases are examples of recent U.S. escape-clause actions. The new FTA standards will reduce significantly the number of cases involving imports from several countries where Canadian exports have been sideswiped, even though they represent an insignificant per-centage of total imports. The FTA also provides new formal procedures for notification and consultation before safe-guards measures can be imposed. Either country has the opportunity to challenge the imposition of a duty or a quanti-tative restriction imposed by the other country under the

FTA "Institutional Provisions." Canada's major complaint in the 1986 shakes-and-shingles case was that the prime minister was not notified of the U.S. president's decision to impose a 35% duty on imports from Canada. In future, the Canadian government will have the opportunity to challenge any such action by the U.S. government before a binding, binational, arbitration panel. The ability of an arbitration panel to make a final decision that is binding on both governments is a unique achievement in international law.

Critics have argued that in the area of dispute settlement Canada has not achieved its fundamental objective in the trade negotiations — security of market access to the United States. This argument is predicated on the assumption that Canada's primary objective was to seek complete exemption from U.S. trade laws. The critics are wrong for the following reasons.

First, the dispute-settlement mechanisms are probably the least important means of obtaining greater security of access to the U.S. market. Tariff reductions, rules of origin, and reduction of non-tariff barriers, such as import and export restrictions, discriminatory technical standards, and government-procurement practices, will do more to enhance the flow of trade between Canada and the United States. Trade disputes represent only the tip of the iceberg and do not affect the majority of business that flows between our two countries.

Complete exemption from each other's trade laws was not a realistic or even sensible goal in the negotiations. Canadian and U.S. anti-dumping, countervailing-duty, and safeguards laws are based on the GATT as well as the 1979 anti-dumping and subsidies codes, and are essentially similar in most ways. Although Canadian businesses tend to be less litigious than their U.S. counterparts, there have been more Canadian anti-dumping investigations involving U.S. products in the last six years than U.S. cases involving Canadian products.

Most experts would agree that the trade laws need to be reformed. There are good economic arguments that in a free-trade area, anti-dumping laws will become irrelevant. Also, many experts have argued that the trade-distorting effects of subsidies could be more effectively addressed by developing a subsidies code, including lists of prohibited and acceptable subsidies as well as new procedures for monitoring and enforcing these rules. Again, no trade expert has seriously suggested that countervailing-duty laws be abolished without replacing them with another system. It has long been recognized within the GATT that subsidies can have trade-distorting effects and should in some cases be disciplined. However, disputes have arisen over what types of subsidies are trade-distorting and should be prohibited, and what types of subsidies do not distort trade and may be used by governments for important public policy objectives.

Unfortunately, reform of the anti-dumping and countervailing-duty laws proved to be too difficult and contentious for the negotiators in the short time they had available. Although both countries were receptive to the idea of replacing the anti-dumping laws with domestic-competition and anti-trust laws, neither country was willing to make significant commitments to change existing subsidy practices. Also, both countries recognized the hurdles involved in trying to obtain the compliance of provincial, state, and municipal governments in any binational regulation of subsidy practices.

The international regulation of subsidies has been, and will continue to be, a thorny issue in Canada-U.S. trade relations as well as in the GATT. The 1979 Subsidies Code is ambiguous, precisely because of the paradox that although most countries recognized that subsidies can have trade-distorting effects, subsidies are widely used by most governments as instruments of domestic policy. In the bilateral negotiations, it was the United States that voiced strong objections to limiting its sovereignty in providing government assistance to U.S. businesses. The compromise struck in October 1987 represents the most to which either country could agree in this sensitive and important area.

There has also been some controversy about whether the decisions made by the binational panels will really have a binding effect. Critics have suggested that a binational panel's decision cannot be binding unless it is capable of being enforced in the domestic courts. This criticism stems from a lack of understanding about international agreements and how they work.

International agreements cannot be enforced like domestic contracts, but this does not mean that a country can ignore its international obligations. International agreements or treaties contain obligations and commitments between countries that are valid as international law. Because of the sovereign nature of the parties, the methods for enforcing these international legal obligations are different from those used for domestic law. Obviously, Canada could not levy a fine or put the president of the United States in jail if the United States fails to live up to an international obligation. However, Canada may have a right to be compensated or to retaliate with measures of equivalent effect if the United States should abrogate a term of an agreement. In international relations, it is often the *threat* of the other country taking retaliatory action that encourages a country to honor its international obligations. As in nuclear relations, deterrence plays an important role in maintaining harmony in international trade relations.

Critics have also suggested that the binational-panel procedures are too fragmented and will not result in continuity and consistency in decision making. This is a serious and important criticism. Many legal observers would have preferred a more integrated, authoritative, permanent, independent institution like the International Joint Commission that administers the Canada-U.S. Boundary Waters Treaty. However, fundamental concerns about sovereignty prevented the establishment of such an agency. As well, the development of an authoritative, international tribunal would raise serious constitutional issues in both the United States and Canada.

The establishment of a Canada-U.S. Trade Commission with the ability to appoint binational panels to resolve disputes was the most to which Canada and the United States could agree in the circumstances. The FTA, however, is an evolutionary document. It is contemplated that the dispute-settlement mechanisms will evolve over time into an integrated, authoritative, independent, international agency. The binational-panel system will be the important first step to developing a new system of trade laws between the two countries.

CHAPTER 10

Why Business Supports Free Trade

It is a puzzle that the debate in Canada about the economic benefits of the Canada-U.S. Free-Trade Agreement (FTA) has largely ignored the strong business support for the deal. The private sector pushed the federal government into the negotiations in the first place. In 1983 the Canadian Manufacturers' Association reversed its century-old support of tariffs and made a submission to the Macdonald Commission arguing for a bilateral trade agreement. Other business groups, large and small, endorsed this concept in many submissions to Ottawa over the 1984–86 period.

Throughout the trade negotiations of 1986–87 the leaders of the business community participated actively on the federal government's new trade advisory committees. The Sectoral Advisory Groups on International Trade (SAGITs) had regular meetings with Canada's Trade Ambassador Simon Reisman and his officials in the Trade Negotiations Office. The shape of the final deal reflected their suggestions and advice, particularly in the exemptions for agricultural marketing boards, all cultural industries, the beer industry, and in the continuation of the auto pact. The SAGITs were also

Alan M. Rugman is Professor of International Business, Faculty of Management, University of Toronto. Further details, in addition to supporting evidence and references for the substantive points made in this chapter, can be found in his recent study *Trade Liberalization and International Investment* (Economic Council of Canada, 1988).

influential in determining the phase-in periods and other aspects of adjustment.

The government's senior advisory group, the International Trade Advisory Committee (ITAC), met regularly with the minister of international trade, key negotiators like Mr. Reisman, and senior bureaucrats. The ITAC prepared detailed position papers that were influential in establishing the parameters of the final deal.

Through this formalized process of ITAC and SAGIT representation, in addition to the usual ongoing informal structure of lobbies and networks, the private sector basically got what it wanted in the final text of the Canada-U.S. FTA. Virtually all leading Canadian business groups, including ones representing small business, were quick to endorse the agreement. And no wonder, since it was *their* deal. Other groups represented on the private-sector advisory committees, such as the Consumers' Association of Canada, also endorsed the deal.

In the light of the perceived need for a bilateral trade agreement and the endorsement by the private sector of the actual deal, why are Canadians apparently still divided on the merits of the FTA? If the business community can live with free trade, does this not demonstrate that there will be economic benefits for the nation as a whole? After all, these private-sector companies provide most of the jobs and generate most of the wealth in Canada.

The enthusiasm of business leaders suggests that they believe that their companies can adjust to the new free-trade environment and that the nation will prosper. Indeed, this is what private-sector leaders are now saying repeatedly on public platforms, in their annual reports, at conferences, and to the media. Many companies have even begun a dialogue with their employees to discuss the benefits of the FTA.

The enthusiasm and commitment of the private sector to the FTA leads to an inescapable conclusion: if business, both large and small, believes that this is a good deal for Canada, then it must be. Even the banking industry, which did not benefit as much as it would have liked in terms of its relative competitive position under the deal, has endorsed the overall agreement as good for Canada and therefore good for the banking business. Similarly, individual companies in protected sectors such as textiles and apparel, which face the greatest potential adjustment costs, have endorsed the principles of the deal and said that they are prepared to seek new opportunities in an expanded North American market.

Opposition to the Canada-U.S. trade negotiations and the resulting FTA has been led by leaders of most of the country's labor unions and by some old-fashioned nationalists, many of whom seem to be ignorant about the most basic facts of modern international business. The opposition of organized labor could be expected because of their vocal commitment to socialist dogma. It is clear that the FTA is based on arguments of economic efficiency and the realities of a competitive global business system. It is also apparent that a socialist focus on distributional goals, which generally conflict with considerations of market forces and efficiency, makes it difficult for those who believe in state planning to support free trade.

What is somewhat surprising is that Canadian nationalists have teamed up with organized labor in their opposition to free trade. Labor leaders are backward-looking in their love of protectionism and fear of free trade. Business leaders are forward-looking in their recognition of the power of global integration and international competition.

Modern Canadian nationalists must wake up to the realities of the world economic system and not continue to dream about yesterday. Canadian workers have been badly served by their union leaders, since their jobs and the prosperity of Canada are tied into the success of the private sector. Canada's labor leaders should ask themselves why socialists in European nations such as Sweden support trade liberalization and the development of multinational enterprises.

Opponents of free trade have ignored the European model and recently advocated an alternative — an industrial policy for Canada. This is antiquated nonsense. An interventionist and protectionist industrial policy cannot succeed for an open-trading economy such as Canada. The call for an industrial strategy is really the protectionist infant-industry argument that has been around for nearly two hundred years. Only large, almost self-contained economies, such as Japan and the United States, can operate potentially successful, strategic trade policies, where the state works with business to promote export industries and restrict imports.

Yet today there is strong evidence that state support for industry promotes inefficiency. This is particularly true in industrialized democracies where sunset industries lobby for protection and achieve it on more occasions than the state can pick winners and develop sunrise industries. The only significant exception in recent times to these harsh realities of competitive global economic life is Japan. However, Japan is a special case due to its cultural and political systems — significant differences that mean Japan is not a suitable model for Canada to follow.

The private sector in Canada learned a painful lesson in the recession years of the early 1980s: no country is an island in an integrated global economy. Canada's production, distribution, and service sectors are all affected by other nations and by rival firms. The stock-market crash of October 1987 emphasized the integration of world financial markets. Today, the world's business is increasingly dominated by large, multinational enterprises and internationally active banking corporations. This worldwide economic and financial integration means that Canadian business needs to be globally competitive. The bilateral FTA is step one toward opening up Canada for efficient international business. Step two, a complementary policy, is to seek multilateral trade liberalization through the current General Agreement on Tariffs and Trade (GATT) round.

This two-track policy of bilateral and multilateral trade liberalization was started by the federal government in 1986 and continues to be its policy. The GATT was never an alter-

native to Canada-U.S. free trade; it was always a complement. The private sector long ago recognized this dual trade
policy and it has actively supported both sets of negotiations.

The ITAC and SAGITs have been involved in both the
bilateral and multilateral trade negotiations, although during
1986–87 most of their time was spent on the bilateral, given
the deadlines of the U.S. "fast-track" process. Currently these
committees are helping to formulate policy for the GATT
Uruguay Round.

How Business Will Adjust to Free Trade

Even before the Canada-U.S. FTA was signed on January 2,
1988, forward-looking Canadian corporations started to factor this into their strategic planning. It was apparent that the
environment for international business would be changed by
this major trade deal. Strategic planners regularly assess such
external environmental changes and design internal strategies
and structures to accommodate such changes. By predicting
such changes the risk to the firm is reduced. Appropriate
policies can be formulated and implemented to minimize the
costs of adjustment.

Corporate adjustment to the bilateral trade agreement has
already been eased by the participation of more than three
hundred chief executive officers and presidents in the negotiations as members of the ITAC and SAGITs. These meetings
provided a useful two-way flow of information and the companies were able to recognize the government's strong commitment to the trade initiative. The meetings of these
committees with trade officials and ministers over the last
two years also helped to build issues of adjustment into the
FTA itself. In this interactive process many of the potential
adjustment problems of Canadian corporations were identified and often steps were taken to minimize adjustment costs.

For example, corporations that face real adjustment costs
can be helped by government in two major ways. First, they
can benefit from long phase-ins before new trade regulations

become effective. Second, they can receive direct financial assistance in the form of low-interest loans and other subsidies to help restructuring and plant relocations.

In general, the Canadian government has worked with the private sector to ensure that the FTA contains provisions for the first method of adjustment assistance. One illustration of this is that the FTA cuts all bilateral tariffs to zero by the end of a ten-year period. Yet industries that volunteered were able to secure quicker tariff reductions; the final text of the FTA reflects many examples of such phased tariff reductions.

As a result of the consultative process plus the nature of strategic planning, corporate adjustment to free trade is already underway. Few of Canada's large corporations will be hurt by the FTA; most will benefit. Canadians should applaud the ability of our corporate leaders to seize this opportunity to organize for future prosperity.

This focus on the strategic planning of large corporations is, of course, justified since most economic activity is carried out by such firms. Indeed, in terms of Canada-U.S. trade the great majority of all international transactions are undertaken by multinational enterprises, much of this by about fifty companies with sales of a billion dollars or more. These members of the "billion-dollar club" consist of a set of Canadian-owned multinationals such as Northern Telecom, Alcan, Noranda and Nova, in addition to a set of foreign-owned subsidiaries such as General Motors of Canada, Ford Canada, Canadian General Electric, DuPont Canada, and so on. These firms are already well positioned in terms of global competitive strategy and the impact of the FTA on them will be neutral to favorable.

These large multinationals are already integrated across the Canadian-U.S. border. Often they made initial plant-location decisions based on the need to secure access to either the Canadian or U.S. markets in the face of barriers to exporting. Now, however, there are other motives for their foreign activities. Virtually all of these multinationals continue to produce and distribute through foreign subsidiaries due to managerial motives such as the need to service customers, to be close to suppliers, to accommodate local political interests, and so on. Stated more formally, most of these multinationals have erected entry barriers that they naturally want to maintain against potential rivals.

The major impact of the FTA on the billion-dollar club is simply to improve the investment climate. This is achieved by having the rules of the game in place, instead of being subject to arbitrary changes through the process of decentralized administered protection, as occurred in the use of U.S. trade-remedy-law cases in recent years. The binational-appeal body for the dispute-settlement mechanism should lead to more objective analysis by the trade agencies, the negation of frivolous cases, quicker decisions, and an overall improved trade climate. The elimination of such uncertainty is the essence of good strategic planning. Therefore, the larger multinationals will benefit from this and related aspects of the FTA that improve market access.

There are two other types of Canadian corporations that need to be considered. First, there are small and medium-sized businesses producing in Canada and exporting to the United states. Clearly these firms will benefit from secure and relatively open access to the U.S. market. Small business is immensely better off when compared to the alternative, which was increasing U.S. protectionism through the use of often capricious U.S. trade-law procedures and other regulations affecting Canadian exports. For this reason small business should benefit most from the FTA.

Second, there are corporations in import-competing sectors that will need to adjust to free trade. However, here the adjustment process will be minimized since most of these sectors were represented on SAGITs and, at their request, they were exempted. Examples of exempted sectors include agriculture, the cultural industries, and the beer industry. In agriculture all the marketing boards were maintained and quotas retained to keep out foreign suppliers as tariffs are lowered. Even in textiles and apparel, steps were taken to minimize the adjustment problem by long phase-ins, discussion of special provisions on duty remission for imported fabric from third countries, and related measures.

Some of these exemptions have raised problems for intermediate producers such as food processors. Now they will be facing U.S. competitors but they could end up paying more for agricultural inputs due to Canada's retention of marketing boards. The food processors seem to have two alternatives: either obtain access to the allegedly cheaper U.S. suppliers or take action to remove some of Canada's interprovincial barriers to trade in the form of marketing boards.

For food processors and some other intermediate producers such as auto-parts makers, the FTA represents an unfinished agenda. But the underlying nature of Canada's internal federal system, with its resulting economic inefficiencies, could not be solved in an external commercial treaty. Perhaps the FTA can supply the incentive to clean up our act at home?

The firms that are vulnerable to free trade are inefficient ones, often sheltered by government policies. However, these firms are on thin ice in any new trading environment, including one reformed through the GATT. For example, many breweries are of uneconomic size due to provincial regulations that were not affected by the free-trade deal. Yet the beer industry and related types of firms protected by such interprovincial barriers to trade will remain vulnerable to GATT actions and eventual competition from more efficient rival firms. This is not an adjustment problem caused by free trade; rather it is one caused by the lack of free trade. The implication of this analysis of the issue of corporate adjustment is perhaps surprising to opponents of free trade who are unaware of the realities of modern international business. There is no adjustment problem for efficient firms.

The Seventy-percent Rules

As the business community in Canada has strongly supported

the FTA, what does it know that apparently half of the public does not? Business understands the two new principles of Canadian economics — the seventy-percent rules.

The first seventy-percent rule is that 70% of all Canadian-U.S. trade is conducted by multinational enterprises. This is easy to understand when we remember that fully one-third of all bilateral trade is in the auto industry, which is still dominated by the Big-Three U.S. auto multinationals.

Also, as is becoming increasingly better known, in the last few years Canadian-owned multinationals and Canadian entrepreneurs, like Robert Campeau and the Reichmann brothers, have been moving aggressively into the U.S. market. Therefore, today, there are massive two-way flows of investment and trade between the United States and Canada, most of it done by the fifty large multinationals.

These multinational enterprises have already served to integrate the U.S. and Canadian economies. Now the FTA will simply reinforce this trend and thereby ensure steady growth for these corporations. However, in terms of public policy, one implication of this is often ignored: there will be few adjustment costs. With 70% of trade already being handled by U.S.- and Canadian-owned multinationals, there is little risk in the FTA. The multinationals can readily adapt to the rules of free trade, incorporating these into their strategic planning.

The second seventy-percent rule is that today 70% of all jobs in Canada are in services. This is the sign of a wealthy and mature economy. Canada long ago moved on from having most of its people in the fur trade, in agriculture, in resource extraction, or even in manufacturing industry. Today the most valuable, and highest paid, jobs are in services. The older professions of law, medicine, and so on have been overtaken by a vast growth of Yuppies working in financial services, health care, education, and other managerial and administrative jobs. Services also include jobs in fast-food chains, but those are only a small part of the picture. Mature, wealthy economies such as Canada's demand a variety of sophisticated consumer and producer services, most of which are increasingly well paid.

Business leaders understand that the jobs of this 70% of Canada's people are not even at risk under the free-trade deal. If business knows that it can adjust to free trade then the Canadian economy will prosper, maintaining a growing demand for services and for people working in service industries. Many of these jobs require training and education; as a nation, Canada has first-class educational institutions already producing such human capital. The role of the education sector will expand under free trade. Business should also help to finance the expansion of both general and specialized educational facilities, the ultimate source of a nation's competitive edge. It is in the self-interest of business to do so but the result is a social benefit that sustains the growth of well-trained Canadians.

The conclusion on corporate adjustment is that the FTA will have a relatively limited adverse impact on jobs and economic welfare. Business, small and large, can handle the adjustment issue on its own. The FTA is basically a commercial arrangement, liberalizing barriers to trade and investment. It is not a threat to Canadian sovereignty, nor the end of the country. It is good business and sound economics. The private sector wanted the FTA and, as it can handle the adjustment issue itself, all Canadians should become more prosperous in the future.

CHAPTER 11
Employment Effects

Among the most emotive issues surrounding the "great free-trade debate" have been the assertions and arguments by both sides on the jobs that will be gained or lost as a result of the Canada-U.S. Free-Trade Agreement (FTA). Various studies have purported to show either very large increases in the number of the jobs in Canada due to free trade, or alternatively, a large number of job losses. It is the purpose of this chapter to discuss how these studies come to the conclusions they do, offer some judgment as to the reliability of these estimates, and put the jobs issue in perspective. The economics of employment is an old and difficult subject; it is also a subject in which controversy is routine.

The Job Loss/Creation Process

Before addressing the quantitative studies, it is important to put the general issue of jobs and the FTA in the broader perspective of economic policy and the job loss/creation process in the modern economy. Since the Great Depression,

Richard G. Harris is Professor of Economics, Queen's University, Kingston. Some supporting references for this chapter are provided in the author's "Jobs and Free Trade," in *Ontario Trade at a Crossroads: Options for New International Agreements* (Ontario Economic Council, 1985), and various articles on the subject in the *Free Trade Monitor*, a periodical publication by the C.D. Howe Institute. Other critical supporting references include *Work and Pay: The Canadian Labour Market*, vol. 17, of the Royal Commission on the Economic Union and Development Prospects for Canada (Ottawa: Minister of Supply and Services, 1985.)

governments have taken full employment as one of the goals of economic policy, if not *the* goal. Success has been mixed in the postwar period, and some economists are of the view that government actually has little impact on the job creation/loss process. Macroeconomic stabilization policies, using both fiscal and monetary policy, are the tools one typically thinks of as being used to affect the number of employed in the short to medium term. It is somewhat ironic that the free-trade debate has focussed on the FTA as either a creator or loser of jobs, since it is not the policy tool one would normally direct to job creation. Indeed, in the classical discussion of trade liberalization, jobs per se receive very little attention. Trade liberalization is seen as a means to greater specialization, improved productivity, higher incomes, and lower consumer prices.

On the other hand, protection is a policy often motivated by the attempt to preserve jobs in the protected sector, by shifting the cost of this job protection on to taxpayers and consumers. Numerous studies have documented the extraordinarily high cost of this type of job protection. The protection argument is often turned around to demonstrate that the *removal* of existing protection will create job losses. This often is true, but not always. Usually such arguments fail, however, to note that the removal of protection creates income in the economy, which creates jobs elsewhere. In the event of a *bilateral* trade liberalization, the removal of barriers to both countries' exports creates additional jobs and income. The question then is really twofold:

- Who will lose their jobs and for how long will they remain unemployed?

- Where will jobs be created and at what level of wages?

A balanced assessment of any trade agreement must address both questions.

In attempting to answer these questions one must recognize the rather limited extent to which a trade agreement is likely to actually affect the functioning of the labor market over both the medium and longer term. First, normal employment changes associated with the business cycle are likely to be far larger than any changes due to reductions in tariffs or to a few plants either opening or closing. Exogenous shocks to the economy through changes in the terms-of-trade (a fall in raw materials prices, for example), the appearance of new international competition (Taiwan and Korea, for example), financial shocks such as the Crash of '87, or large changes in exchange rates — all have a much greater impact on jobs than will a trade agreement that involves gradual reductions in barriers over ten years and provides improved market access.

Many people are surprised to learn that jobs are routinely created and destroyed at an incredible rate within the Canadian economy. Individuals move into and out of unemployment frequently. Some of these periods of unemployment are voluntary, taken to search for a new job, for example. The large flows of people between jobs, and between jobs and periods of unemployment, are staggering. Some estimates, for example, suggest that as many as one out of four Canadians changes jobs in a given year.

There is no evidence to suggest that the FTA is going to change the turnover dynamics of Canadian labor markets to any great degree. Most studies either focus on the impact of the FTA on the stock of existing jobs, or on the longer term effect on the stock of employment, or the unemployment rate. In the same vein it has been pointed out by numerous labor-market observers that demographic and industrial changes have had a far larger impact on jobs than trade liberalization. The increased participation rate of women, the continued growth of the service industries, and technological change have been affecting employment in a number of ways. Yet among the Organization for Economic Cooperation and Development countries, Canada has one of the most impressive records of job creation in spite of, or perhaps because of, this ongoing structural change.

In asking whether any economic policy is going to create or destroy jobs, it is important to ask, "Relative to what alternatives?" Two points in this particular debate are worth making. The first concerns possible U.S. protectionism and the role the FTA may play in mitigating future U.S. protectionism against Canadian exports. Most studies do not compare the FTA against an alternative of increased U.S. protectionism. Yet there is little doubt that an increase in U.S. protectionism would have a rather dramatic both short- and medium-term effect on the number of jobs within Canada.

The second point concerns the relevant phase in the business cycle during which the FTA is implemented. Central Canada is currently in a state of over-full employment by anybody's calculation. There is little prospect that employment will be created in the next two years by the FTA. If the FTA was initiated during a recession, it would be another matter. In the resource-based provinces, unemployment remains above the levels of the 1970s but improvements there have been noticeable. The FTA should have some employment impact in those sectors but the high capital intensity of resource industries will limit these gains.

The FTA and Job Loss/Creation

Turning now to the studies that attempt to quantify the job gains and losses, these fall into roughly four categories. The first set of studies are sectoral-specific studies based on surveys of firms conducted by industry associations, consulting firms, academics, or government departments. Firms are asked questions as to how they will respond to the FTA. Questions about investment, exporting, pricing, product quality, and employment are used to make inferences as to the likely impact of the FTA on the particular sector in question.

The second class of studies seeks to define the relevant domain of competition induced by the FTA. Generally, industries or product lines are defined as potentially competitive or non-competitive vis-à-vis the U.S. competing product, and then the studies go on to assess the number of "jobs at risk."

The third set of studies are those that use quantitative economic models that focus on what I will crudely call "aggregate demand impacts" of the FTA. These studies are considerably more sophisticated than those previously referred to and deserve careful scrutiny.

The last set of studies incorporates supply-side effects into a supply/demand framework. Often these analyses are longer term and are concerned with the supply of various skilled-worker categories in particular industries and regions. In general it would be desirable to define jobs in relation to occupation, industry, skill level, region, and perhaps by sex. Most of the studies have not done this, simply because of time constraints or the lack of data. I shall discuss each of these methodologies in turn.

The sectoral studies have been for the most part what one would expect from such qualitative and impressionistic surveys. Many firms seem quite confident that they can compete in their own industry. Others feel that significant export opportunities may emerge under the FTA. Specific sectors such as financial services, high-technology sectors, some processing industries, and the conventional export-oriented industries have conducted studies showing a favorable response to free trade. Others have been less favorable, depending on who was doing the surveying. Because most of the information in these studies is collected from businessmen, the studies are subject to the criticism that there is a bias in favor of the FTA induced by a pro-free-market outlook of business. Most do not actually contain any hard forecasts on job loss or creation.

The second class of studies estimates the number of products and industries that are, broadly speaking, import competing. Studies conducted for the Ontario government, the Ministry of Employment and Immigration, and a number of the trade unions fall into this category. They each come to the conclusion that either the number of jobs defined as subject to potential competition from U.S. firms are "at risk" or will be lost. This basic approach is at best meaningless. First, there is a sense in which all the jobs in manufacturing and a large share of the services sector are potentially competitive with foreign competition. By these methodologies, for example, the number of jobs that would have been lost or at risk under either the Kennedy or Tokyo Round tariff reductions of the General Agreement on Tariffs and Trade (GATT) would have included the entire work force in the manufacturing sector of Canada.

There have been some traditional economic studies of what might be called the impact effect of domestic removal of protection for countries, including the United States and Australia, for example. My own attempts to use this methodology have led to the conclusion that the FTA would cause far fewer job losses than the "potential-competition" methodology would suggest.

In making such estimates, the worst-case assumption is to assume that wages in the industry are fixed; thus, all reductions in demand for domestically produced goods result on impact in the loss of employment, assuming rigid technology. In such an exercise the key parameter is what is referred to as the elasticity of substitution between competing imports and domestically produced goods. The higher this elasticity, for a given market share of imports and a given percentage tariff reduction, the larger the decrease in demand due to the increased demand for foreign goods.

There are two things to note about this parameter. First, most statistical studies have suggested that in the short run (less than two years) it has a value in the range of 0.5 to 1.0. With a tariff reduction of, say, 10% and a market share of imports of, say, 50%, a reduction in the tariff from 10% to zero *immediately* would yield a reduction in the demand for the domestically produced goods of between 2.5% and 10%. This decrease in demand would, under the worst-case scenario, yield equivalent industry employment reductions.

In the case of Canada-U.S. trade the numbers are going to be even smaller, first because most tariffs against U.S. goods are less than 10% and in many cases the market share of imports is considerably less than 50%. This type of impact calculation on job loss, however, will most likely overstate the job losses, simply because it ignores exchange-rate adjustment. If the impact effect induces an increase in imports such that the current account deteriorates, the result would be a depreciation of the currency that, in turn, would serve to restore competitiveness of the dometically competing industries.

Most impact studies have failed to ask the question of how long the initial period of unemployment is going to last. In work done on the effect of the Trade Adjustment Assistance Act in the United States, it was found that the period of unemployment in import-competing industries following a tariff reduction was surprisingly short for most workers, usually less than three months. Barring the onset of a recession, I think it is reasonable to expect similar results for Canada, and suggest that the impact approach may be seriously flawed as a way to focus on even the short-term adjustment to the FTA.

Some of the impact studies have raised other issues. At the top of the list is the possibility of large-scale movement of production, for example, the closing of branch plants or, alternatively, the sudden shift of resource processing from Canada to the United States. There is virtually no economic evidence supporting these views. Under previous tariff reductions most branch plants began the process of rationalization, and there are few remaining that serve only the domestic Canadian market. Those that do are in the most protected sectors of the Canadian economy.

Experience suggests that a more likely outcome is that a parent company would choose to produce at the existing location a more specialized set of product lines, rather than simply to close the plant. Of course, in the event that Canadian production is not efficient even after rationalization, there is good reason to be rid of such inefficient plants, since they would only perpetuate a low-skill, low-wage set of employment opportunities.

The second point made by some of these studies is that job losses may be concentrated among women. The case is made, for example, in the textile and clothing industries where the low-skill jobs at risk are held in large share by women. It must certainly be admitted that if large-scale reductions in demand come about in these sectors, then a higher proportion of women will lose jobs than men. However, the basic proposition that these industries are going to be losers under Canada-U.S. free trade is debatable. Work done by my colleague David Cox and myself suggests that both clothing and textiles could be significant beneficiaries, both from reduced Canadian protection and improved access to the U.S. market. While the capital intensity of production is likely to rise as modernization and rationalization proceeds, the scenario of large-scale job losses in these sectors is unlikely.

From the broader perspective, the logic that trade liberalization will cause undue job losses for women relative to men is false for one simple reason. Most jobs for women are in the service industries relative to manufacturing. In 1983, 61% of the jobs in services were held by women. Job losses will be borne almost entirely on impact in the manufacturing sector, where men hold 72% of the jobs, and the positive income effect of free trade will be felt principally in the service sectors, which account for more than two-thirds of the existing jobs. Over the longer term, job gains will be shared among both men and women. However, to predict who will benefit relatively more is difficult if not impossible.

Another set of studies attempts to quantify both job gains and job losses through the use of economic analysis that focusses on demand side effects. In addition to the job-loss effect of import penetration referred to above, these studies include the job-creation effects of increased exports and the impact on aggregate demand of additional income created through trade liberalization.

Most of these studies have come out of traditional macroeconomic models used for the analysis of monetary, tax, and fiscal policy. The results of these studies are uniformly positive on the view that the FTA will lead to an increased number of jobs. The most notable of these studies was carried out by the Economic Council of Canada, which predicts 300 000 additional jobs over a ten-year period. Other macroeconomic models from private sector, government, and academia have come to similar conclusions.

These studies point out the extreme importance of taking a balanced view of trade liberalization. The positive effects of increased exports has a traditional multiplier effect on domestic income that offsets the income losses on employment in those sectors suffering reductions in output through loss of markets share to imports. In Canada because the share of exports to gross national product is so high, greater than 30%, the multiplier effect of increased exports on aggregate income or gross national product is quite significant.

Most of these studies, however, are somewhat controversial because of additional assumptions made on productivity and investment. These assumptions are made exogenous to the model and affect the results in obvious ways. For example, it is typically assumed that productivity will improve and investment will rise as a result of the FTA. These assumptions, while entirely plausible and consistent with the evidence from microeconomic-based studies, are judgmental inputs to the analysis.

More problematic, however, is that these studies, by focussing on the demand side, tend to ignore the supply side constraints in the economy. Thus, both increases and decreases in demand across sectors of the economy translate into changes in employment and output, rather than changes in wages and prices. For this reason they probably paint a picture on balance that is slightly more optimistic than is warranted.

Supply-Side Considerations

On the supply side of the issue, longer term analysis of the employment effects of the FTA must recognize that basic supplies of skilled labor are variable over the longer term, through changes in the population, immigration policy, participation rates, and a host of education and training factors. The FTA itself may do little to affect these structural factors. What can be said is that the demand for high-skill jobs in manufacturing and resource industries will likely increase at the expense of low-skill jobs. Ultimately this will mean that the gap in wages of skilled workers over low-skilled workers will increase. Canada should, over the longer term, end up with more skilled workers, if the Canadian labor-market institutions respond adequately to the pressures of increased international competition, including those produced by the FTA.

In the short to medium term, however, supply side effects in the labor market are likely to be quite important. Those export industries that expand will largely be those that are already, or are about to become, competitive, and hence predominately use skilled as opposed to unskilled labor. In addition, the indirect demand for labor induced in business services, transportation, and financial services will be predominantly for skilled, as opposed to unskilled, labor. It is my view that there is not an excess supply of skilled labor currently available in Canada. Thus the increased demand in those industries and sectors should lead to a rise in the real wages of skilled workers and not to an increased number of jobs.

In work done for the Select Committee on Economic Affairs of the Ontario Legislature, I looked at the problem of jobs from the supply-constrained perspective, but allowing for job losses in import-competing sectors. My conclusions were that the aggregate job gains would be positive, but considerably less than the 300 000 jobs forecast in some of the demand-side-oriented calculations. It is even possible that the job gains under some scenarios could be virtually negligible.

In general, the picture seems to be that the FTA would have a very small impact on the total employment/unemployment picture. Of course, this conclusion may be unduly pessimistic because of the presumed supply constraints and because it ignores possible investment induced in Canada through a confidence effect, as a result of the FTA being signed. Other serious, but as yet unresearched, supply constraints are likely to emerge as a result of specific imbalances between the existing occupational composition of the work force and the particular occupational demands induced by the FTA.

From the perspective of analysing the impact of increased protectionism by the United States on Canadian jobs, the supply-side issues are of little relevance. Reduced exports to the United States would result in job losses across all sectors, both import-competing, export-oriented, and the service industries. The short-run effects would be quite devastating in terms of aggregate employment and income. For example, a 15% across-the-board tariff by the United States against Canadian exports could raise the unemployment rate anywhere from between five to fifteen percentage points, depending on the response of wages, interest rates, and the exchange rate to the increased protection. Those who defend the FTA on the grounds that this is what is being avoided certainly have good reason to worry about the effect of U.S. protectionism.

Conclusions

The impact of the FTA on jobs within Canada is most likely to be positive over both the medium and longer term. Impact studies that have focussed on the role of U.S. exports as job displacing in Canada, without taking account of the appropriate price and wage responses within Canada, are methodologically flawed and offer little serious guidance as to true job losses or even the likely pattern of adjustment within Canada. Detailed sector-specific studies, while interesting, offer some insights as to how companies might respond on impact to the FTA but are of little use in predicting job gains or losses.

Quantitative economic analysis suggests that, from a demand-side perspective, there are good reasons to be optimistic about the net job-creating effects of free trade. Improved market access, more efficient plants, plus reduced protection of domestic industries, all lead to an increase in both exports and imports so that, on balance, the net job-creation effect of the FTA would be positive.

The view that job gains will be large, however, must be tempered by supply constraints in Canadian labor markets, particularly for skilled workers. If these supply constraints are significant, the aggregate job gains are likely to be smaller, with a larger share of the gains from the FTA showing up as higher wages to skilled workers rather than as an increase in the number of jobs.

CHAPTER 12
Women as Winners

Public opinion surveys conducted over the past year have indicated that a significant gender gap exists in Canadian attitudes toward free trade with the United States. Women are less likely than men either to support the Canada-U.S. Free-Trade Agreement (FTA) or to consider free trade a positive development for Canada.

There are several possible explanations. The Ontario government, through its Women's Directorate and other anti-free-trade lobbyists, have been very effective in creating the impression that Canadian women have reason to fear free trade. Free trade's impact on women has been the focus of many of the most confused and uninformed arguments characterizing the debate, ranging from the threat of U.S. recruitment of Canadian women as candidates for surrogate motherhood, to the elimination of Canadian social programs, to the possibility of large-scale takeover of day-care centres by profit-hungry U.S. enterprises.

In fact, free trade will bring substantial benefits to Canadian women, both as consumers and as workers. The consumer gains arising from free trade are particularly relevant since women generally spend a greater share of their incomes

Katie Macmillan is a policy analyst at the C.D. Howe Institute, Toronto. Ms. Macmillan is the author or co-author of various publications, including *Focus on Follow-Through, Policy Review and Outlook* (Toronto: C.D. Howe Institute, 1988), *The Canadian Common Market: Interprovincial Trade and International Competitiveness* (Calgary: Canada West Foundation, 1985), and *Free Trade and Canadian Women* (Ottawa: Canadian Advisory Council on the Status of Women, 1987).

on basic necessities, the prices of which are often higher as a result of Canadian tariff and non-tariff barriers. On the employment side, the job gains arising from free trade will vastly outweigh any losses that will occur. Most of the new jobs created will be in service industries, where female employment is already heavily concentrated. Consequently, women are well positioned to gain from the job expansion that will occur.

The employment gains from free trade have particular relevance for women since they provide an opportunity to redress some of the basic inequalities women currently face in the workplace. On average, Canadian women earn two-thirds the wages of men and they are poorly represented in those occupations offering the highest incomes and most promising career opportunities.

While many of the causes of gender-based inequalities in the workplace are sociological in nature, one can consider the extent to which economic policies have contributed to or exacerbated these disparities.

There is little doubt, for example, that the brunt of protectionist trade policies is borne by Canadian women, not only as consumers but as workers. When tariff and non-tariff barriers create jobs in the import-competing manufacturing industries, it is often women who take these positions. These are probably the least attractive jobs the economy has to offer in terms of wages, working conditions, skill levels, and opportunities for advancement. Contrary to what anti-free traders maintain, most women workers probably would choose not to stay in these occupations if offered an alternative, and would not recommend them to their daughters.

The major achievement of a free-trade agreement with the United States would be the replacement of poor jobs in protected industries with better jobs in expanding sectors. The effect of existing protectionist policies is to freeze women in low-paying positions until these jobs are finally eliminated through competition with Third World countries.

This chapter will consider the impact of free trade on

women as workers and women as consumers. Free trade's influence on social institutions and policymaking in Canada is discussed in the final section of the chapter.

Women as Workers

Opponents of free trade maintain that tens of thousands of female jobs will be lost under free trade. In fact, considering where female employment is concentrated, women are not nearly as vulnerable as has been suggested.

More than four-fifths of Canadian women in the labor force are employed in the services sector, and the majority are in industries referred to as non-traded services, including education, health care, public administration, and personal and business services. The jobs of these workers and those employed in the primary sector of the economy are not threatened by free trade with the United States. Free trade will not mean that Americans will deliver our mail, teach our children, or nurse our sick. Virtually all of these sectors are exempt from the FTA, which leaves the Canadian government free to regulate them, to discriminate between Canadian and U.S. operators of these services, or to establish government monopolies to provide them wherever desired.

Numerous studies, including one by the Economic Council of Canada, predict that substantial employment gains would arise under free trade with the United States. Service industries, in particular, will benefit from increased spending and investment by Canadian consumers and businesses, who will have more income available as a result of the economic expansion accompanying a move to free trade. The Economic Council of Canada has predicted that four service industries — retail and wholesale trade, and commercial, personal, and business services — would account for 65% of the new jobs created in the entire economy by free trade, or as many as 225 000 jobs. Women currently represent 56% of the employment in these particular industries, compared to only 26% of employment in the manufacturing sector.

Less than 12% of the Canadian female labor force is employed in the manufacturing sector, which is where the bulk of trade-induced adjustment will occur. The Ontario government, using some very questionable techniques, predicts massive job losses for women in manufacturing. This prediction is based on the observation that a significant share of female manufacturing employment is concentrated in those industries considered to be the most sensitive to trade pressures.

There are many problems with the Ontario government's insinuations. First, it is misleading to suggest that women will be disproportionately affected. Male jobs in those so-called "trade-sensitive" industries outnumber female jobs by almost two to one. Insofar as adjustment will be required in these industries, the numbers suggest that almost twice as many men will be affected.

Second, free-trade opponents are frequently guilty of confusing general import sensitivity with sensitivity to free trade with the United States in particular. Although these industries may be at a competitive disadvantage vis-à-vis Asian countries such as South Korea, Taiwan, or Japan, indications are that many of these same manufacturing industries could survive and even prosper under a free-trade regime with the United States. U.S. tariffs, which are high in the same industries, would be removed under the FTA and the phase-in period would be as long as ten years for heavily protected industries. The effects of tariff reductions are expected to be small compared to other pressures faced by Canadian industry, such as technological change and exchange-rate fluctuations.

The textile industry bears particular mention in this regard, since some fear that the industry would virtually disappear if tariffs against the United States were removed. The Canadian textile industry has gone on record in support of free trade and has demonstrated its confidence in its ability to compete in the U.S. market by undertaking substantial capital investments in the past two to three years. The bilateral

FTA provides for annual quotas on textiles moving between the two countries, thus preventing an import surge in either direction. Both countries would maintain external tariffs against third nations, which is where the bullk of competition arises. Trade disruption is expected to be minimal and the free-trade environment could provide the chance for Canadian firms to improve their competitive position within a larger but still relatively sheltered market.

Some adjustment to free trade is inevitable and it will probably affect those women least advantaged in the Canadian labor market. Any losses that will occur will be greatly overshadowed by the new jobs created — jobs that offer more promise for the workers involved. In any case, the overall adjustments arising from free trade are expected to be minimal compared to the job-switching that occurs as a matter of course in the Canadian economy. Ronald J. Wonnacott, in a recent study for the C.D. Howe Institute, estimates that as much as 4% of the Canadian labor force changes jobs every month. The stereotype of the factory worker employed at the same job for thirty years is not as true as many believe.

The issue is not whether job loss and job creation is a good or bad thing; clearly, it goes on all the time. For Canadian women the relevant questions are what difficulties does labor adjustment pose and how can adjustment work to their advantage?

New evidence, based on labor-force surveys conducted by Statistics Canada in the late 1970s and early 1980s, challenges traditional views on women and job loss. The survey findings suggest that, on average, women workers who have lost their jobs are unemployed for shorter periods of time than men and, in contrast to men, experience an increase in earnings when they move to a new job. In many respects, this reflects the fact that women have nowhere to go but up. If women can improve their circumstances because of job change, however, then job change is not an entirely bad thing.

Labor mobility and skills-upgrading programs can help women workers make the transition from poorer jobs in declining industries to better jobs in growing sectors of the economy. Women are typically underrepresented in existing programs, however, and generally benefit to a much lesser extent than men from skills-upgrading initiatives. Greater sensitivity to the special characteristics and requirements of women is necessary when designing and implementing job-skill programs in Canada. It is through the achievement of better job skills, not through trade protectionism, that women can improve their status in the workplace.

Women as Consumers

Trade barriers raise consumer prices and limit access to items available in the international marketplace. This lowers the standard of living for Canadians because consumers must devote more of their income to pay for what they require.

High tariff and non-tariff barriers particularly hurt women, since a greater share of their incomes tend to go toward the purchase of basic necessities such as food, shelter, and cloth-ing, which are made more expensive as a result. For example, the tariff on most children's clothing items imported from the United States is currently 25%. If the FTA is implemented, this tariff will be completely eliminated over ten years.

Factors that influence the cost of basic necessities have great significance for the incidence of poverty. Poverty is overwhelmingly a female phenomenon in Canada, with 2.8 million women and children, or 71% of Canada's poor, living below Statistics Canada's low-income cutoff line.

It is frequently asserted that there will be no consumer savings arising from the removal of trade barriers between Canada and the United States. While reliable estimates are difficult to arrive at, significant savings are bound to occur. To deny this displays an inconsistency often found in the arguments against free trade — that industries will both lay off workers because of increased competition but will be able to maintain or increase selling prices in spite of that competi-tion. Simply put, if one claims that free trade will not affect prices, then one is also saying that Canada will not face the job adjustments to which opponents of free trade so often refer.

Free Trade and Social Policy in Canada: Some Misconceptions

Many of the most extreme arguments against free trade centre on its impact on social institutions and social policymaking in Canada, areas of particular concern to women. The issues raised by those opposed, however, tend to display a lack of understanding both of the FTA itself and of the scope for independent policy action.

Critics of free trade claim, quite mistakenly, that the FTA would open our child-care centres to takeover by U.S.-based enterprises. In fact, child-care and other government-provided services such as health, education, and social services are among those explicitly excluded from the services section of the FTA. This means, in effect, that the two countries can continue to discriminate between U.S. and Canadian providers of these services and can establish government monopolies excluding all private provision, if desired.

In Canada, the regulation of child-care facilities is a provincial government responsibility, with the result that quite distinct child-care systems have evolved in each of the provinces. The FTA itself affects neither the quality nor quantity of child-care operations in Canada, nor the ability of the provinces to regulate these operations. The same is true of education, hospitals, and other services provided by governments in Canada.

It is often claimed that free trade will eventually force Canada to dismantle programs such as medical plans and unemployment insurance, and preclude Canada from introducing initiatives, like pay equity, that are not already in place in the United States. Not only are programs of this nature excluded from the FTA but also they would not be subject to countervail or other trade actions by the United States, provided they are universally available.

One of the most important factors distinguishing Canadian society from that of the United States is Canada's strong public commitment to the well-being of its citizens. Canada's ability to provide generously for disadvantaged Canadians is something that has been preserved in the FTA with the United States.

To the extent that universal social programs raise the cost of doing business in Canada, this would be reflected in Canada's exchange rate. A lower dollar vis-à-vis the U.S. dollar helps to maintain Canadian competitiveness when trading with the United States, in spite of Canada's more developed social safety net.

Interestingly, the greatest threat to Canadian programs in the health, education, and social areas probably stems from domestic factors. As Canada enters an era of aging population and greater demands for public services, expenditures on these items are likely to be constrained more by lack of funds than by trade pressures. The economic growth generated by a freer trading environment would have positive consequences for government revenues, thus making it easier to meet or increase Canada's commitments in the social policy field.

Conclusions

Free traders and those opposed have different views on how women will improve their economic circumstances in the years to come. Critics of free trade envisage a system of trade protection, financed by Canadian consumers, enabling women to remain in industries in which Canada has great difficulty competing in the global marketplace. Those in favor of free trade see it as an opportunity to create better jobs for women workers, thus reducing their dependence on what are often the worst jobs Canada's economy has to offer.

Free trade offers Canadian women the potential to

improve their economic standing, both relatively and absolutely. Virtually every analysis on the subject that makes a systematic appeal to evidence concludes that the FTA would expand Canadian incomes and create employment opportunities. While some job losses would occur, women have demonstrated capacity to adjust to, and even profit from, changes in the workplace. Labor mobility and upgrading programs can help women to adjust to the better opportunities that free trade will generate. Women can be winners from free trade by using the changes that it brings to permanently improve their economic status.

CHAPTER 13
Labor Market Adjustments

While the bilateral Canada-U.S. Free-Trade Agreement (FTA) may be expected to create substantial long-term benefits, it will impose costs on those who are dislocated and have to switch jobs.

The most important mechanism for bringing about an adjustment in this area is the operation of private firms and labor markets. Wherever tariffs have been reduced — whether in the formation of the European Community or the Kennedy and Tokyo Rounds of trade liberalization — rising wages and employment opportunities in expanding export sectors have drawn labor and other resources from contracting, import-competing sectors. Canadian business and labor have a proven track record of remarkable resilience and capacity to adjust to this sort of challenge. An estimated 4% of the employed Canadian labor force is separated from its jobs every month, and about 25% every year. At the same time,

---

Ronald J. Wonnacott is Professor of Economics, University of Western Ontario, London. With his brother Paul he has written numerous books and articles on Canada-U.S. economic relations, including the effects of free trade. He also has written a number of books on statistics and econometrics with his brother Tom. This chapter draws heavily on the first three chapters of R.J. Wonnacott and Roderick Hill, *Canadian and U.S. Adjustment Policies in a Bilateral Trade Agreement*, (Toronto: C.D. Howe Institute, 1987), which also provides the source for the estimates cited here and presents a detailed evaluation of present Canadian adjustment-assistance policies.

since total employment has been rising, even larger numbers have been finding new jobs.

The government has been playing an important supporting role in this adjustment process, and there are three broad reasons why it should continue and expand this responsibility in any move to bilateral free trade.

Why Government Assistance Is Required

The most important reason is *equity*. It is only fair that some of the net benefits to society from bilateral free trade should be used to reduce the burden on those individuals who face dislocation and thus have to bear the cost of this policy change.

The second reason is *efficiency*. Although private markets play the key role in the adjustment process, they do not always operate efficiently in all respects. And when they do not, government action may improve their performance. For example, private firms and individuals tend to underinvest in human capital, and this justifies government assistance for retraining programs that upgrade Canada's stock of human capital. From the point of view of efficiency, it is also important to concentrate on programs such as retraining and relocation assistance that increase the capacity of the economy to adjust, rather than programs, such as income grants well above those provided by unemployment insurance, that may deter adjustment by reducing the incentive of the unemployed to find new jobs.

The third reason for government assistance is *political efficacy*. It may be impossible to sell a policy of liberalized trade unless adjustment-assistance programs are in place. An example is the most straightforward of all adjustment policies: delaying the elimination of tariffs by phasing them out over time. Protection is temporarily continued to provide business and labor with breathing space and an opportunity to adjust to the new set of circumstances.

For all three reasons — equity, efficiency, and efficacy —

there is an important role for the government to play in providing adjustment assistance.

Putting the Problem into Perspective

The large adjustments in the past (reflected, for example, in
the 4%-per-month separation statistics cited earlier) have been
in response to pressures *other* than the FTA. Since these pressures — that is, these other sources of employment shock —
will have to be faced with or without a free-trade agreement,
they are worth considering in detail.

Much of the adjustment required by Canadian producers
will be in response to domestic pressures, such as increases in
supply from newly established firms; changes in consumers'
tastes; technological change that makes new products available; and/or cost-cutting innovations in production processes, such as recent microelectronic advances that have
revolutionized computer-aided manufacturing systems.
Although these shocks are classified as domestic, they could
equally well come from a foreign source. For example, large
increases in supply may come from foreign rather than
domestic firms.

Dramatic improvements in communications and transportation, along with multilateral reductions in trade barriers
under the Kennedy and Tokyo Rounds, have left foreign producers no longer at a distance but instead right at our door-
step, offering their highly competitive products. The
resulting increase in trade has provided enormous benefit
since Canadian consumers can now choose from a wider
variety of products at lower prices. While Canadian producers have benefited from increased access to foreign markets,
they have also had to adjust to increased competition from
imports in the Canadian market. This challenge will be
increased to the degree that the current Uruguay Round is
successful in liberalizing trade further.

Pressures from increased foreign competition have come
from several directions.

- Highly developed, high-income countries including Japan and a number of nations in Europe now have the capacity to innovate that allows them to compete in the most advanced and sophisticated products.

- The newly industrializing countries (NICs), including South Korea, Spain, and Brazil, are now challenging North American producers in many basic heavy industries such as autos and steel. For a country like Brazil that has financed much of its dramatic development by international borrowing, the heavy payments it now faces on its debt increase the pressure on it to export more, and this raises the level of its competitive challenge. Just as resource-poor Japan has traditionally been forced to be hypercompetitive in manufactured goods in order to finance its unavoidable resource imports, now some of the NICs like Brazil must become hypercompetitive in manufactured goods in order to service their debt.

- Many developing countries such as Malaysia, the Philippines, and now even China, have been moving toward labor-intensive, light manufactures, such as textiles. In particular, recent Chinese improvements in agricultural productivity have allowed them not only to reduce their traditional imports of agricultural goods, but also to divert labor and other resources from agriculture into an expanding manufacturing sector. Thus China now raises a new competitive challenge for North American producers of both agricultural and manufactured goods.

Such shocks from changing foreign competition have been very significant. They represent one of the important influences on exchange rates, and these rates have been fluctuating dramatically.

How Serious Will the Adjustment to Bilateral Free Trade Be?

To the above long list of foreign and domestic adjustments

that Canadian producers will have to face in any case, the FTA will add another: the necessity of adjusting to Canada-U.S. tariff removal and the lower-priced imports from the United States that will result. How important will this be, relative to the others?

Although this appears to be a difficult, if not impossible, question to answer, there is one important clue that strongly suggests that the answer may be "Not relatively large." The reason is that exchange-rate fluctuations reflecting other shocks — including the foreign shocks described above — have been running as high as 10% or more per year. These fluctuations can be expected to exert a greater effect on the competitive position of producers in Canada (and thus on the pressure to adjust) than will the planned, phased-in reduction in bilateral tariffs of 1% to 2% per year or less that the FTA provides for in most industries. Therefore, the FTA can be expected to add only another tier to the more substantial adjustments Canada will have to face in any case. And there are three reasons for expecting that this additional tier will not be excessively difficult to accommodate.

- Studies of Canada-U.S. free trade, along with the experience of the European Community, suggest that much of the adjustment will take place *within* industrial sectors rather than between them. Indeed, much of the adjustment will take place within firms, as they develop new products and marketing capabilities to take advantage of new trading opportunities.

- Although increased imports from trade liberalization will put downward pressure on Canadian employment, increased exports to the United States will put upward pressure on Canadian employment. Historical experience suggests that, when both of these pressures are taken into account, trade liberalization tends on balance to increase employment in participating countries, with perhaps the best indirect evidence coming from the Great Depression in the 1930s when rising levels of protection were a major reason for falling employment. Moreover, Canada-U.S. free trade will tend to have a further positive effect on manufacturing employment in both countries precisely because it is a *bilateral* agreement: industrial production in each country is likely to be stimulated by the preference each would grant to the other. To illustrate, suppose the United States now has a 10% tariff on an item that is imported from Canada and Italy. Under tha FTA, Canadian producers will be able to export this to the United States duty-free, and thus enjoy a 10% preference over Italian exporters who will still have to pay the 10% U.S. tariff.

- While it can be argued that the FTA will, on balance, increase Canadian employment, there is an even stronger expectation that it will have a favorable employment effect *when compared to the relevant alternative of no FTA* — and it is in this sense that the term "favorable employment effect" will hereafter be used. With no FTA, there would be far greater risk that increasing U.S. protectionism would damage Canadian exports and employment, with no offsetting expectation of job increases of the kind offered by the FTA. This is critical because the Canadian economy is so dependent on trade with the United States. About 20% of Canadian gross national product — and consequently a substantial percentage of Canadian jobs — is generated by exports to the United States. As a specific example of great importance for Ontario, the FTA should provide a reasonable degree of stability to auto trade and employment. Without the FTA, the United States would be likely to take action against Canada on auto trade, with the big question being whether this would reach into the auto pact, and if so, how far, and at what cost to Canadian employment.

Conclusions

The FTA will add another tier to the more substantial set of adjustments that Canada will have to face in any case. But because it is likely to have a favorable effect on employment, the FTA should make *all* adjustments less painful, including not only bilateral free-trade adjustments, but also the other foreign and domestic adjustments that will have to be faced in any case. The reason is that a lower rate of unemployment not only reduces the number of individuals without jobs, but also it reduces the cost faced by each because the average duration of unemployment is less. With a low unemployment rate, workers get other jobs quickly, whereas in periods of high unemployment when they have to join a long queue, they have to wait longer for a job.

Moreover, it should be emphasized that the relatively favorable effect on employment is a special bonus provided by the FTA. This policy would be beneficial even if it had no net short-run effect on employment. The reason is that, like technological change, the FTA is designed not to increase employment, but rather to increase efficiency, labor productivity, and income. Moreover, like technological change, the FTA will make the Canadian economy more competitive, and thus increase its ability to create high-productivity, high-income jobs in the future. Such jobs should be of particular interest to those, including many women, who now earn low incomes. It is an opportunity for them to upgrade their productivity and income by taking advantage of government programs to retrain them for these better jobs.

A related conclusion is that the currently fashionable exercise of counting jobs at risk from bilateral free trade is not particularly helpful. Instead it provides a seriously biased picture because it does not recognize adequately — if at all — that

- Many of these jobs are at risk because of other foreign and domestic pressures that cannot be escaped

- Many of the jobs at risk, given present comparative costs, will not be at risk if Canadian producers can use their new access to the U.S. market to scale-up and reduce their costs

• Many jobs will be saved and created by this policy

To reject the FTA on this basis is like keeping word processors out of an office because you can count the jobs that would be put at risk. Or, more dramatically, it's like saying "No" to the Industrial Revolution because in those days one could easily count the jobs at risk, but not the higher-income jobs that were eventually created. In the case of Canada-U.S. free trade, it is easier to identify many — but not all — of the jobs that will be created because they are in existing export industries.

Even though trade liberalization can be expected to have a favorable effect on the number and particularly the quality of jobs, it will involve job switching, and this is often painful for those individuals involved. Therefore, the government will still have a responsibility to provide adequate adjustment assistance. Moreover, even in a period of job switching when the number who get new jobs exceeds the number losing them, some individuals will be left unemployed. This will be a particular problem for those who will be beyond the age at which they can be retrained and re-employed. In such cases, the government has a special responsibility to provide assistance, for example, in the form of subsidized early retirement.

Two concluding observations: the flexible Canadian dollar will provide a safety valve to help keep Canada competitive in the unlikely event that the country does run into substantial problems in adjusting to Canada-U.S. free trade. For example, if Canada encounters difficulty in exporting and in competing with imports, then the Canadian dollar will fall, thus reducing Canada's problem in competing.

Finally, adjusting to bilateral free trade now will make the Canadian economy more competitive and will thus increase Canada's ability to adjust to other shocks in the future. And that should be Canada's ultimate goal in a world in which domestic and foreign changes are occurring at an increasingly rapid rate: to develop an economy that will adjust to shocks from *any* source. The adjustment to bilateral free trade should be viewed as simply one necessary step in that process.

CHAPTER 14
Social Policy and Regional Development

Since neither regional-development incentives nor social programs are "traded," they are not even mentioned in the Canada-U.S. Free-Trade Agreement (FTA). Therefore, the status quo prevails, or as the federal government puts it in the explanatory notes accompanying the text of the FTA: "Canada's capacity to pursue regional development and social welfare programs remains unimpaired."

Over the medium term (five to seven years), however, the FTA may impact more directly on the nature of socioeconomic and industrial policies in both countries, particularly in the regional-development area: the two countries will attempt to develop a set of mutually agreeable rules in relation to government subsidies and other anti-competitive measures, with a view to replacing the present arrangements relating to countervail and anti-dumping.

Despite the fact that social programs and regional-development initiatives have been left out of the FTA, in public debate and in the popular press, concerns about the future of social and regional policy have been anything *but* left out. Included front and centre in assessing the "Sale of Canada Act," as some critics refer to the FTA, is the claim that Canada will inevitably turn back the clock on its impressive post-

Thomas J. Courchene is Roberts Professor of Canadian Studies, York University, Toronto. Portions of this chapter draw on the author's recent monograph, *Social Policy in the 1990's: Agenda for Reform* (Toronto: C.D. Howe Institute, 1987).

war achievements on the social and regional policy fronts. Variants of such claims appear almost on a daily basis. My view is that these claims are entirely without foundation.

For one thing, the manner in which Canada finances certain social policies (e.g., health plans, old age security) bestows a very substantial advantage on Canadian industries, so that there will be no *internal* pressure to alter these programs. And since these programs are national in scope they are inherently non-countervailable. Therefore, it is difficult to see where or how *external* pressure will arise. For another, the FTA provides exactly the sort of economic environment within which the bulk of the remaining initiatives on the social and regional fronts will become substantially more effective — an argument for intensifying, not reducing, efforts in these directions.

Underlying these observations are two rather fundamental points. First, if Canada attempts to meet world competition constrained by a domestic market of 25 million, it is much easier to make the case that a leaner and meaner social-policy network is needed to offset this market-size disadvantage. This argument disappears with an FTA. Second, there will be employment and real income gains associated with an FTA that will both reduce the costs of social programs (since Canadians will be moving from unemployment insurance or welfare to employment) and make existing social programs more affordable.

Competing Constitutional Visions

Nevertheless, because the full ramifications of the FTA are not well understood, it is entirely legitimate, indeed encouraging, that Canadians are concerned about the future of their social programs. In order to place this concern in a more appropriate light, it is instructive to draw on Jeffrey Simpson's recent insightful article, "Choosing the Lesser of Two Evils" (*The Globe and Mail*, October 9, 1987). Simpson casts the underlying differences in the citizen/state relationship in terms of the two countries' respective defining constitutional rhetorics — "peace, order, and good government" for Canada and "life, liberty, and the pursuit of happiness" for the United States.

History, culture, language, geography, and a sparse population have all played a role in developing among Canadians a more benign approach to government and a heightened concern for collective rights, in sharp contrast to the individualism that is the hallmark (more so recently, under Reagan) of the U.S. creed. Even the Canadian Charter of Rights and Freedoms (while arguably very "Americanizing" because it transfers power to individuals, via the courts, thereby introducing a checks-and-balances feature into Canada's previous Parliament-is-supreme approach to governance) differs from its U.S. counterpart in that it enshrines aspects of collective rights — sexual-equality rights, aboriginal rights, multicultural rights, and soon perhaps, the "distinct society" of Meech-Lake fame.

However, nowhere do these dueling paradigms appear to apply with more force than in relation to the two countries' approaches to social and regional policy. On the social policy front, Canada's publicly funded and administered health-care system stands in sharp contrast to the more individualistic or market-oriented U.S. approach.

The contrast is even more evident on the regional front: although the United States engages in very extensive regional policy on the expenditure side (e.g., defence contracts), the United States has nothing that even comes close to Section 36 of the Constitution Act, 1982. Section 36(2) requires Parliament to ensure that all provinces have access to sufficient revenues (via equalization payments) such that they can provide "reasonably comparable levels of public services at reasonably comparable levels of taxation" while Section 36(1) commits both levels of government to reduce regional disparities in opportunities and, more generally, to promote equal opportunities for the well-being of all Canadians. Neither of these collective-rights aspects features prominently in

U.S. policy. Indeed, it is not evident that the U.S. Constitution would even allow such regional-specific initiatives.

Despite these acknowledged and entrenched differences, concerns remain and are compounded by the reality that the FTA, with its enhanced emphasis on markets, resonates more, as Simpson notes, with life, liberty, and the pursuit of happiness than it does with peace, order, and good government. Therefore, the underlying issue can be rephrased as follows: Is the FTA with its express market orientation in terms of allocation likely to overwhelm the more sharing and collective-rights approach of Canadians on the distribution front? From my perspective, the answer remains a confident "No."

Policy Evolution and the FTA

Prior to focussing on some specific programs in the social and regional field, one further issue needs to be addressed. Proud as Canadians may be of their social-policy accomplishments, the fact remains that there are pressures throughout the western world to re-integrate social and economic policy. In Canada's case, the basic social-policy network was designed to address the challenges of the prosperous 1960s. This it did admirably well, but the recent flurry of initiatives at both levels of government suggests that further evolution in the social-policy system is inevitable if Canada is to meet the challenges of the 1990s.

My own writings in this area argue that the new social-policy challenges relate to the mushrooming fiscal burden, to the enhanced competitiveness emanating from the world economy, and to the emerging needs on the social-policy front (e.g., the aging of the population and the changing role of the family, as reflected by the number of single-parent families in the work force). In terms of the traditional trade-offs in the system, addressing these challenges will probably require that the evolution will be in the direction of favoring adjustment over entrenchment, favoring a greater reliance on ability to pay rather than on universality, and in some, but not all, areas favoring decentralization over centralization. Others may, of course, disagree. However, the critical issue is *not* what Canada's social-policy framework will look like in 1999, but rather how much, if any, of this will be *the direct and inevitable result of the FTA*.

In this context, many Canadians focus on the recent federal day-care initiatives as evidence that the FTA will erode our social-policy fabric. Setting aside the positive aspect of this initiative (i.e., that it is the only new shared-cost program to be inaugurated in the last two decades), I recognize that many Canadians would prefer that day-care be uniform across the provinces and that it exclude the possibility of private-sector provision. At base, this has nothing to do with the FTA: rather it is a lament that Canada is a federation, not a unitary state, and that day-care is a provincial responsibility. Therefore, criticism should be directed against Section 92 (provincial powers) of the Constitution Act, 1867, and not against the proposed FTA.

Social Policy

For the purposes of this chapter, social policy is defined to encompass the range of policies and programs designed to maximize the opportunities for Canadians to enhance and employ their human capital. I will deal in turn with policies related to post-secondary education, employer-financed social programs, and health and income supplementation (welfare).

Canadians are placing much emphasis and, more recently, a reasonable amount of funding, on human-capital formation, research and development, and technology, and, in particular, on the notion that, increasingly, Canada's competitive edge in the world economy must come from the country's knowledge base. Given Canada's history, it is perhaps not surprising that Canadians are experiencing some difficulty in making the transition from a resource-based culture (i.e., "If we don't cut it or gut it or dig it — we don't do it.") to a research- or human-capital-based culture. However, complicating any cultural barriers to this are trade barriers — tariffs, quotas, and a protectionist environment tend in general to enhance the *last generation's skills*. If Canadians maintain this inward-looking stance, they should not be surprised that their biggest export will eventually be human capital. Required here is a willingness and a confidence to challenge the world head-on in the knowledge-based sector which, in turn, implies opening Canada's economy to freer trade.

In general, investment in human capital and research and development is a natural winner under free trade. Not only will the returns to such investment be enhanced (and the incentives increased for educated and skilled Canadians to remain in Canada), but with secure access to the U.S. market Canada now stands to benefit to a far greater degree from the whole process of technology transfer.

Turning now to the general issue of policy sovereignty, it is instructive to focus on the recent tax-reform exercise. In my view, Canada had little choice but to follow the United States in decreasing corporate tax rates. If Canada's rates were to remain substantially higher, both domestic and foreign multinationals would simply have transferred profits to the United States (to take advantage of its lower corporate tax rates) and transferred deductions such as interest payments to Canada (to take advantage of its higher rates to maximize the value of deductions). The net result would have been a dramatic erosion of Canada's corporate tax base. Therefore, given the integrated nature of the two economies Canada had little choice but to follow the United States, *quite independent of the FTA*.

In terms of employee contributions to social benefits, I argued earlier that removing the competitive disadvantage associated with access/market size would diminish any pressures for scaling down in this area. Others have argued the opposite, namely that an open border will enhance the ability of Canadian business to pressure governments to erode Canadian social benefits.

Some data will show that this latter scenario is highly unlikely. Based on payroll data for manufacturing (from the National Product Accounts for the United States and from unpublished Statistics Canada sources) employer benefits account for about 11% of payroll in Canada and 17% in the United States. If one excludes unemployment insurance and workers' compensation payments (which are slightly higher for Canada), the employee shares of pensions and health and life insurance are about 7½% in Canada and 14½% in the United States. On the pension side the difference arises because the Canada Pension Plan is not as yet fully matured, and because the Old Age Security Pension and the Guaranteed Income Supplement payments are funded out of consolidated revenues. On the health and life insurance side, health insurance is clearly the major difference. There may well be cases where firms in some locations in the United States can avoid some of these charges, *but on a national-average basis Canadian firms enjoy an overwhelming (and non-countervailable) advantage here*.

Where will the pressure for change come from? One answer might be from firms that end up as losers under the FTA. However, paring down employer-related financing of social programs is a very inefficient and ineffective way of assisting those Canadians that may suffer under free trade. In general, therefore, I see little or nothing to be concerned about here in terms of Canadian social programs.

Canadians view their medical- and hospital-insurance system as a sacred trust. As noted above, the nature of Canada's health-care financing bestows a substantial cost advantage on Canadian industry. Moreover, the Canadian system is more efficient than that in the United States, as measured by costs as a percent of gross national product. Finally, it is inherently non-countervailable. So, who among Canadians will cast the first stone? It is correct to note that the competitive advantage that health insurance bestows on Canadian auto makers was emerging, prior to the FTA, as a major U.S. concern in terms of the auto pact. With the FTA, however, this issue is diffused, not heightened.

The evolution of Canada's welfare and income-support system is in full swing and quite independent of either the prevailing U.S. model or the FTA. The provinces, led by Quebec, are becoming very concerned about the "poverty traps" that are created by the current system, for example, situations where the "full" tax rate (including expenditure benefits) in the transition from welfare to employment typically exceeds 100%. Several provinces now provide various versions of earnings-supplementation programs for the working poor. Moreover, under federal tax reform, most tax deductions have now been converted to credits. The obvious next step is to make these tax credits refundable. When this occurs (and it will be soon) Canada will be well on its way toward a negative income tax or an income-tested, guaranteed annual income.

It is true that the work incentives in such a system are consistent with free trade, so that the impact of the FTA may be to hasten its arrival. However, the building blocks have long been firmly put in place both at the federal level (with the introduction in the late 1970s of measures like the refundable child tax credit) and at the provincial level (with wage-subsidization programs for low-income individuals and families), and this evolution will proceed with or without the FTA.

Therefore, I find suggestion that the FTA will overwhelm Canada's social policies difficult to fathom. Moreover, it is not clear just how this undermining of Canada's long-standing and firmly entrenched social philosophy is supposed to come about. One frequent argument is that it will result from a gradual altering of Canadians' social mores, as more trade begins to flow north-south rather than east-west and in the process Canadians become more "Americanized." But until recently the largest two-way flow of international trade in history was between Ontario and the United States (only

very recently surpassed by U.S.-Japan trade). Have Ontar-
ians, as a result, abandoned the Canadian traits of greater
sharing and a larger role for government in the social-policy
area? Pay equity, among other things, is clear evidence that
they have not. Why should it be different for Manitobans or
Nova Scotians if the FTA allows them to engage in more
north-south trade?

Regional-Development Initiatives

By far the most important point to emphasize in terms of the
interaction between the FTA and regional policy is that the
FTA itself is, apart perhaps from equalization, the most significant regional-development initiative in the postwar era
and perhaps ever. Consumers will obviously benefit (e.g.,
real incomes will increase). The resource sectors (e.g., energy
in the west and Quebec and fishing in the east) are also clear
beneficiaries. Moreover, by opening up north-south trade the
FTA addresses in one fell swoop both the distance and
market-size burdens of the regional economies (i.e., their cen-
tre-dominated peripheral destiny within Canada).

In turn, this leads to a second and very important aspect.
With the advent of the regional-development agencies, which
transfer more control over regional development to the
regions themselves, the opportunity now exists for the regions
to direct these new initiatives in a manner consistent with
capitalizing on and enhancing the gains that will derive from
the FTA itself. All in all, a very upbeat picture.

Turning now to the future of regional initiatives under the
FTA, the first point to note is that the bulk of Canada's commitments on the regional front are enshrined in the Constitution and, therefore, they transcend the FTA and even an
abrupt about-turn by Canadians in relation to regional sharing. However, the FTA may constrain the manner by which
Canada *implements* certain regional initiatives. For example,
in the event of another energy-price spike, the FTA effectively constrains Canada (thankfully) to use the tax-transfer

system rather than the price system to redistribute energy rents. But the FTA does not constrain the *goals* that Canadians set for regional policy.

The FTA and Countervail

In terms of countervail under the FTA, the status quo prevails — what was countervailable pre-FTA remains countervailable post-FTA, with the important caveat that these disputes will now go before the new, and presumably more objective, binding, binational panel. However, both Ottawa and the provinces have long recognized that high-profile subsidies targeted to an exporting plant or industry will maximize the likelihood of countervail measures. Governments remain free, pre- or post-FTA, to subsidize or provide incentives for specific industries that produce for the domestic market, and they may also have considerable leeway when it comes to import-competing industries. The essential point is that Canadian governments have been backing away from those regional development incentives that will trigger countervail. The FTA merely entrenches this development.

Second, recent developments on the regional front (e.g., the Atlantic and western agencies) have begun to place less emphasis on boards and mortar and more emphasis on mortarboards. Part of this policy shift presumably reflects the general consensus that the old boards-and-mortar approach has not worked. Part also probably reflects the fact that Prime Minister Pierre Trudeau and the other architects of the Constitution Act, 1982, cast the regional commitment less in terms of physical infrastructure than in terms of equalizing well-being and opportunities for all Canadians. Therefore, to the extent that Canada's regional policies became directed toward providing individuals and communities with this human-capital infrastructure (providing expertise, training, research and development, etc., to facilitate the development, production, packaging, and marketing of regionally based products), the likelihood of countervail diminishes substantially. To be sure, this is consistent with the dictates of the FTA, but the emphasis on putting people rather than things at the centre of regional development is, in my view, most welcome in its own right.

The generalized unemployment insurance program is not subject to countervail since it is a national (i.e., not industry-specific) program. However, a few years ago the United States brought countervail measures against the ground-fish industry. Surprisingly, from my perspective, the United States lost the countervail case. Perhaps it was because the United States focussed its case on the regional aspects of unemployment insurance (which are not specific to the fishing industry) rather than on the fact that fishermen are the only self-employed workers eligible for unemployment insurance. The good news here, I suppose, is that if the fishing component of unemployment insurance is not countervailable (even under the pre-FTA procedures), Canada may well have substantial leeway in terms of regional-development initiatives.

The bad news is that the United States should have won this case for two reasons. First, the self-employed provisions in unemployment insurance for fishing *are* an industry-specific subsidy. Second, while unemployment insurance as an income-replacement program is an essential and integral part of an overall income-security system, that component of unemployment insurance that has as its goal income support or maintenance, rather than income replacement, ought to be folded into a generalized income-support program (i.e., an income-tested guaranteed annual income).

This was the view of the recent Newfoundland Royal Commission on Employment and Unemployment, which argued that the impact of unemployment insurance in the Newfoundland economy among other things: undermines the intrinsic value of work, undermines good working habits and discipline; undermines the importance of education; is a disincentive to work; discourages self-employment; distorts local development efforts; is vulnerable to manipulation, etc.

The underlying point here is not so much to argue that unemployment insurance needs some rethinking but rather to emphasize that if, a few years down the FTA road, Canadians do modify unemployment insurance, this will have little to do with the FTA, per se.

In summary, therefore, while regional disparities will always exist, the FTA represents the best news in a long time for Canada's regional economies.

Conclusions

Finally, as noted above, the FTA provides that over the next five to seven years both countries will attempt to develop a mutually acceptable set of rules relating to subsidies and other anti-competitive measures. The prevailing wisdom in Canada is that this will constrain Canada much more than it will the United States. The opposite is far closer to the truth. If, as I suspect, Canada's new initiatives on the regional-policy front will be more successful than its past forays in this area, Canadians may be quite prepared to agree to such a subsidy pact, since these new regional initiatives represent a movement away from measures that are countervailable to those that inherently are not. In contrast, a substantial number of U.S. states have, over the period of the 1980s, suddenly "discovered" regional-development initiatives in the wake of the rust-belt, sun-belt shift, so that they are likely to be much more difficult to bring into line. Therefore, it is the United States, not Canada, that will probably be the stumbling block on the subsidy code. Advantage: Canada, in this bargaining process.

While it is reassuring that Canadians are concerned about the future of Canada's social and regional policies under the FTA, the fact of the matter is that the FTA critics are dramatically overplaying (albeit effectively, in terms of public opinion) this concern. Where Canada's initiatives on this front are not enshrined in the Constitution they are just as firmly entrenched in Canadian social philosophy. Moreover, this social philosophy has led Canada to finance the bulk of social programs through the general tax system, rather than loading them (regressively) onto industry, which in turn implies a substantial comparative industrial advantage under the FTA. If there are problems with the FTA, they are not to be found on the social- and regional-policy fronts.

CHAPTER 15
Sovereignty: Culturally, Economically, and Socially

The Canada-U.S. Free-Trade Agreement (FTA) offers great advantages, many of which have been discussed elsewhere in this book. "These advantages are all very well," say many of the critics, "but good Canadians will understand that rejecting the FTA is the price of remaining Canadian." They go on to assert that "If we Canadians trade more with the Americans, we will become more like them. We will catch their alleged lack of dynamism and adopt everything from their economic and social policies to their gun laws."

To assess these concerns, we need to look first at the FTA itself, then at the possible effects of the forces that the FTA may set loose.

Richard G. Lipsey is Senior Economic Advisor, C.D. Howe Institute, Toronto. Relevant publications include: R.G. Lipsey and M.G. Smith, *Taking the Initiative: Canada's Trade Options in a Turbulent World* (Toronto: C.D. Howe Institute, 1985); Lipsey and Smith, *Policy Harmonization: The Effects of a Canadian-American Free Trade Area* (Toronto: C.D. Howe Institute, 1986); and Lipsey, "The Great Free Trade Debate and the Canadian Identity," text of convocation address to Carleton University (Ottawa: Carleton University Press, 1987), available from C.D. Howe Institute, Toronto.

Sovereignty and National Treatment

When two or more sovereign nations sign a treaty, they agree to do some things and not to do other things. Thus, it is not a relevant criticism of any international treaty to say that it entails a loss of sovereignty — all treaties do. The relevant question to ask is: Did what we give up and what they gave up constitute a mutually beneficial package?

To understand the issue of sovereignty, we must understand the principle of national treatment, which is enshrined in the FTA. National treatment allows each government to follow any policy course it chooses, and to adopt policies that are totally different from the other government's policies, with only a single important proviso: that the government does not use these policies to discriminate solely on the basis of nationality, either overtly or covertly.

For example, Canada can have high taxes on cigarettes sold in Canada, while the United States can have low taxes on cigarettes sold in the United States, as long as the taxes in both countries apply to both Canadian- and U.S.-made cigarettes. Similar rules apply to standards. Canada can, for example, require that all children's clothing sold in Canada be non-flammable, provided only that the restriction applies both to Canadian- and U.S.-made clothing. At the same time, the United States may permit some clothing to be flammable, as long as the rule applies equally to goods made in both countries.

The same principle also applies to investment. Canada can have any policies in relation to investment, and these can differ by any amount from U.S. policies. Canada can regulate how firms invest, where and by how much they produce, and a host of other things, as long as these rules and regulations apply to all firms, irrespective of whether they are Canadian or American.

The purpose of national treatment is to leave intact the sovereign right of each country to go its own way on all of its policies, *as long as it does not use these policies as disguised barriers to international trade or investment*. How reasonable — and how unlike the horror stories put out by opponents of the FTA that every distinctive Canadian policy would be ruled out under the FTA terms.

The following is what the FTA basically does.

- It applies the principle of national treatment to almost all trade in goods, to many services, to standards, and to some types of foreign investments.

- It then protects current policies in two ways. First, virtually all laws that affect things other than trade in goods are grandfathered, even when they offend the principle of national treatment. This is true for a wide range of policies, ranging from those regulating the export of raw logs to those prohibiting the sale of healthy Canadian oil firms to foreign interests. Second, a range of sensitive industries are *completely exempted* from any national treatment obligation. Examples are day-care, health, education, any Crown corporation, and all cultural industries.

Constraints of Sovereignty under the FTA

There are two main ways in which sovereignty can be affected by an international treaty. First, sovereignty is constrained by the treaty itself in what may be called *direct constraints*. Second, when the agreement is put in place, it may set up pressures that constrain governments in their future exercise of sovereignty. These are "policy harmonization pressures," not directly called for in the FTA, but nonetheless caused by it. These are called *indirect constraints*.

For the two years leading up to the completion of the FTA, those who opposed negotiation asserted that Canadians would be pressured to give up such valued social policies as unemployment insurance and free medical care. In the event, none — not one — of Canada's social policies was bargained away. Furthermore, Canadian negotiators agreed to relatively few restrictions on our sovereignty in relation to economic policy, while all cultural policies were given blanket exemption from the terms of the treaty.

Direct Constraints: What Canada Did Not Give Up

The discussion of national treatment should make it clear that most of the allegations of major losses of Canadian sovereignty are unfounded, even where an activity is covered by FTA. For example, Canada did not give up its right to operate any social or tax policies that differ from those in the United States. Furthermore, cultural industries and all social programs are excluded from the FTA. To illustrate what this implies, consider the important case of child-care. Under the FTA, Canadian governments have more power than many would want them to use. For example, they can:

- have any rules and regulations that they want, to cover all firms that provide such services, both Canadian and American, by virtue of the principle of national treatment established in FTA Article 501

- have different rules applying to Canadian- and U.S.-owned firms, by virtue of the exclusion of child-care and other sensitive services under the Annex to Article 1401

- set up a nationalized service and prohibit any private day-care, whether Canadian or American owned, as provided for under Article 2010.

In view of the clear language of the FTA, the continued assertion that it opens the way for day-care services provided by U.S. firms at an undesirable standard (what might be described as Kentucky-Fried Child-Care Chains) is unfounded.

Many of the other things that Canada did not give up are covered later in this chapter.

Direct Constraints: What Canada Did Give Up

The two main areas where the FTA puts significant constraints on Canadian (and U.S.) sovereignty are investment and energy. Even here, however, Canada gave up very much less than is commonly supposed. Furthermore, little is given up that has not already been given up under the General Agreement on Tariffs and Trade (GATT) and the International Energy Agreement. Our obligations under the FTA are, however, likely to be more enforceable than those under the GATT, and so they may effect some increased restraint on Canadian (and U.S.) sovereignty in practice, even where they do not do so in law.

Energy: Basically, the FTA legalizes the status quo of free trade in energy. Canada gains the enormous advantage of secure access to the U.S. market in return for agreeing on the principles of national treatment in relation to government pricing policies and allocation of supplies during periods of shortages.

The FTA incorporates two existing GATT rules that constrain Canada's energy policy:

- Canada cannot use government policy to impose a different price for our energy products in the Canadian domestic market than in the U.S. market

- in times of severe shortage, Canada must share the available supplies with the United States, according to a formula based on the proportion of the total Canadian production that has been exported to the United States in the recent past.

Investment: All existing laws that violate national treatment in investment are grandfathered, as are those pertaining to energy. National treatment obligations do *not* extend to existing Crown corporations or to procedures for setting up new Crown corporations. Thus, Canada can continue — subject to our international tax treaty obligations — to tax foreign entities differently than domestic, but promises not to make the tax obligations more discriminatory when, and if, the laws are changed. Canada can also tax foreign and domestic firms differently, provided the tax is not meant to discriminate arbitrarily between investors, and that treatment is no less favorable to that accorded one of its nationals (Articles 1602 and 1609).

What is given up in the investment chapter of the FTA is the right to review some types of takeovers and to impose performance requirements on foreign firms newly entering the country. Indirect takeovers — where ownership of a Canadian subsidiary of a foreign-owned company is transferred to another foreign-owned company — can no longer be reviewed. Giving up that right would not seem to compromise any legitimate national objective, since the firms involved are already foreign owned. Also, the threshold for the review of direct acquisitions — the takeover of a Canadian-owned company by a foreign-owned company — is raised from $5 million to $150 million. This undoubted constraint on future policy has caused a storm of protest. However, its importance would seem to be limited given the following:

• Investment Canada has not reviewed a single case in the range from $5 million to $150 million

• about two-thirds of total non-financial capital in Canada is still reviewable under the terms of the FTA, including the large takeovers that are usually the ones that become the object of national concern

Other important changes to Investment Canada rules involve the prohibition of investment-related performance requirements (Article 1603) concerning local content, import substitution, and exportation of a given amount of production. These requirements have not been used since the 1970s and are inconsistent with Canada's GATT obligations, insofar as they affect international trade. In any case, the prohibition is not extended to performance requirements as part of conditions attached to subsidies or government procurement.

Myths about the FTA

There are so many misunderstandings about the content of the FTA that only a small sample can be given here. All of these are taken from newspaper articles or letters to the editors of various publications.

Myth: The FTA has bargained away Canadian cultural policies.

Refutation: The continued repetition of this myth shows that many of the critics are impervious to evidence. Cultural industries have been broadly defined in the FTA and are totally exempted from the national treatment obligations imposed on other sectors of the economy. In any case, subsidies and other measures to support culture, as narrowly defined, were never at risk. Subsidies to operas, symphony orchestras, jazz festivals, Canadian authors, and learned journals remain perfectly acceptable instruments of cultural policy. Favorable tax treatment for filmmakers also seems possible.

What was discussed at the bargaining table was the mass cultural industries, such as radio, television, and publishing. But even here, Canadian measures, such as Bill C-58 (which disallows as a tax deduction, expenses of advertising on U.S. border radio and television stations by Canadian firms) escaped completely. At the last minute, the modest differential in the postal subsidy to high-circulation Canadian magazines was also saved.

The FTA makes only two changes to Canada's cultural policies. First, it ends the use, without payment, of U.S. and Canadian television signals by Canadian cable-television companies. This practice, which some have called international piracy, needed to be changed. Surely it is in Canada's self-interest to move toward rational rules to protect intellectual property at the international level. All countries gain when the rule of law is imposed for copyrights.

Second, although Canada retains the right to force a divestiture of the indirect acquisitions of Canadian subsidiaries in the cultural area, the FTA requires that the foreign subsidiary be bought out at fair market value. Could any fair-minded Canadian disagree?

When all the hype about Canadian culture is discounted, precious little was given up. It is hard to believe that the FTA will affect any significant aspect of Canadian culture one way or the other.

Myth: The cultural community gained unambiguously by being excluded from the terms of the FTA.

Refutation: By demanding — and getting — exemption from the FTA, members of the Canadian cultural community have also denied themselves the benefits. While business and trades people will be able to cross the border freely in pursuit of their business activities, musicians, dancers, and actors will continue to suffer the present serious restrictions on temporary entry to the United States. One can only be impressed with the altruism of Canadian performing artists who gave up what must have been a dream for many — vastly improved access to U.S. engagements — in defence of the profits of the owners of radio and television stations and large distribution journals, which are the main beneficiaries of measures such as Bill C-58 and the postal subsidy.

Myth: The FTA will make it more difficult for the Canadian government to use subsidies as a policy tool for such objectives as regional economic development.

Refutation: Some provincial premiers have used this incorrect allegation as a reason for opposing the deal. In fact, subsidies will be at risk to U.S. countervail actions just as much — no more or no less — than they are now. Surely the FTA should be judged by the balance between its plusses and its minuses, and not on the places where it scores zero. The relevant comparison is how much access Canadian exporters will have with the FTA, and how much they will have without it. On this comparison, there is no doubt that the FTA is the superior alternative.

Myth: Canada must share all its oil and other energy resources with the United States.

Refutation: This is false. A sharing agreement exists only if *Canada* declares a shortage. *Canada makes that decision unilaterally.* Such a shortage is a very rare event, and under all normal circumstances, Canada is under no sharing obligations other than to let market forces operate.

Myth: The price of Canadian exports of energy to the United States cannot differ from prices charged in Canada.

Refutation: This is wrong. Canadian producers, including Crown corporations, can still charge different prices in different markets. All the FTA prevents is government intervention to *impose* price discrepancies.

Myth: Canada can no longer have independent energy policies that are in the Canadian national interest.

Refutation: This fallacy, which has found its way into high-level political documents, editorials and op-ed items, is quite wrong. For example, Canada can tax producers and consumers of oil, and Canada can control the extraction rate, which is the key policy for purposes of conservation. What Canada cannot do is use these policies as disguised ways of discriminating against foreign oil firms.

Myth: The investment chapter of the FTA opens Canada's gas and oil industries to foreign ownership more than they now are.

Refutation: These industries are fully exempted in the FTA (in Annex 1607.3). Furthermore, under FTA Articles 1602.5 and 1602.6, restrictions on who may purchase firms that are privatized are still allowed (e.g., if Petro-Canada were ever to be sold to the public, a restriction that only Canadians can purchase shares would be permitted under the FTA).

Myth: The FTA investment chapter is a one-sided set of Canadian concessions for no gain.

Refutation: As an important investor nation (Canada's stock of investment in the United States is increasing about three times as fast as is the U.S. stock of investment in Canada), Canada must be concerned to establish rules for national treatment of foreign investment. To have managed to quietly establish these rules for Canadian investment in the United States before there is any backlash against the rapidly growing stock of foreign investment in that country, might seem a decade from now to have been one of the FTA's most farsighted measures. Giving up the seldom-used right to review takeovers of middle-sized firms, and to impose performance requirements on newly entering foreign firms, seems a small price to pay for this gain.

Myth: The FTA prevents the federal or provincial governments from nationalizing any industry.

Refutation: Article 2010 shows this commonly held belief to be untrue. For example, subject to reasonable rules of procedure, a provincial government can nationalize its car-insurance industry and confer a monopoly on a provincial Crown corporation.

Indirect Restraints of Sovereignty under the FTA

Almost daily, we hear that Canada will be forced to remove any social or economic policies that are more costly than those in the United States. Otherwise, say critics, Canadian costs will be raised above those in the United States. Canada will then not be able to compete. Canadian firms will leave for the lower-cost sites in the United States and many of Canada's best people will follow.

This harmonization argument has no support either from the experience of other countries or from Canada's own past experience, and little from economic theory. Consider the following points.

First, seventy-one countries — including all advanced industrial nations except Japan and Canada — are currently in regional trade-liberalizing arrangements without having complained of lost policy independence. For example, Holland has a very expensive set of social policies, yet it has been in a free-trade area with low-spending Belgium for fifty years. Sweden also has many high-cost social policies — indeed many more than does Canada — yet little Sweden trades tariff-free with such economic heavyweights as Germany and France. Throughout history, rich countries have traded profitably with poor countries, and high-spending countries have traded profitably with low-spending countries. The evidence from other countries is clear: free trade is not the enemy of diversity in social policy.

Second, the FTA comes close to completing a program started in 1935 when Canada began slowly reducing its very high tariffs. By 1986 approximately 75% to 80% of the tariff protection that Canadian industry received in 1935 had been removed. During that time, Canadian social and economic policies have evolved along lines different from those followed in the United States. If it is true that liberalizing trade causes policy harmonization, then Canadian and U.S. policies should have been 80% harmonized already. The evidence from Canadian history is clear: Canada can establish and maintain its own distinctive social policies, while liberalizing its trading arrangements with other countries.

Third, harmonizing pressures always exist between any two countries' social and economic policies. If tax rates in Canada exceed those in the United States, some Canadian citizens and firms may move to the United States. Note, however, that *these incentives exist whether or not we have free trade*. Many British people have emigrated to the United States to escape high U.K. taxes, in spite of the high tariffs on U.K.-U.S. trade. Similarly, taxes that hold firms' profits below what can be earned in other countries provide an incentive for firms to emigrate, *whether tariffs are high or low*. There are harmonizing pressures between Canada and the United States, but these are related mainly to the ease with which people and firms can relocate — which are unaltered by the FTA — rather than the ease with which goods and services can be traded. There is thus little evidence that the changes contemplated by the FTA will have more than a small effect on harmonizing pressures one way or the other — countless extreme comments to the contrary notwithstanding.

Fourth, any broad-based social policy that increases business costs across the board, as for example does unemployment insurance, brings into play a compensating change in the exchange rate. For example, if Canada wanted to introduce a new measure that raised all Canadian business costs by 10%, this would not destroy Canada's competitive position. Instead, it would tend to reduce the external value of the Canadian dollar by 10%, leaving Canada's international competitiveness unchanged. This is the reason why the very diverse social policies found among today's trading nations can co-exist.

"But," say the critics, "Canada is different from all other nations so that no other country's experience is relevant to our situation." It strikes me as odd that the same people who say Canada is so unique that other nations' experiences are irrelevant, also feel that Canadians are so similar to Americans that we will become American if we trade a bit more with them.

These people tell us that we will lose our distinctive Canadian identity under free trade. Anyone who has lived in the United States knows that Canadians are not like Americans. The reasons for our profound differences lie in our different histories, geographies, and immigrant experiences. We Canadians should have enough confidence in ourselves to grasp the offered material advantages of free trade with the United States, while understanding that we will remain Canadian even if we eat one more McDonald's hamburger or watch one more episode of *Dallas* — or trade a bit more with the United States.

If we do not actually become Americans, we are told that we will catch their alleged lack of dynamism, and adopt their gun laws. But consider Canadians' past experience. The decline of the British economy began around 1890 and continued all through the twentieth century. Britain, however, remained Canada's most important trading partner through the first half of this century, without our catching the British disease or adopting their class system. I suspect I buy my groceries from a monarchist and sell some of my consulting services to a Marxist. But trading with these guys to our mutual advantage makes me neither a monarchist nor a Marxist. We Canadians should have confidence in ourselves. We can rub shoulders with Americans without becoming American.

As for adopting U.S. gun laws and other idiotic accusations, we might as well tell Moslem Pakistan that trading freely with Hindu India will cause it to convert to Hinduism.

The U.S. offer of preferential access to its mass market has made Canada the envy of the trading world. Yet in a fit of national insecurity, Canadians may reject the offer. In my view, we should grasp the historic opportunity, understanding that we have little to lose but our fears.

CHAPTER 16
The Constitutional Dimension

Inevitably, the constitutional question has become a major dimension of the free-trade debate in Canada. The inevitability of this question arises from the fundamentally federal nature of the Canadian nation. It is ironic that Canada, having started out on paper as a highly centralized federation much less committed to federalism than the United States, has become a much more federal country than the United States. With virtually every important public policy initiative, the question of whether it is a subject of federal or provincial jurisdiction gets nearly as much, and sometimes more, play than whether it is a good policy.

In Canada's highly federalized political culture it is the provincial governments, not the federal upper house, that have come to be regarded as the legitimate instruments for representing regional interests in the making of national policy. The Mulroney government recognized this fundamental fact of Canadian political life in its approach to the Canada-U.S. Free-Trade Agreement (FTA). That is why the prime minister and the Canadian negotiating team consulted with the provincial premiers and their governments at various stages in developing the Canadian position. Obtaining the

---

Peter H. Russell is Professor of Political Science, University of Toronto. He is a specialist on constitutional and judicial politics. His most recent book is *The Judiciary in Canada* (Toronto: McGraw-Hill/Ryerson, 1987).

provinces' support for the FTA was regarded not as a legal but as a political imperative.

In the end Ottawa was successful in obtaining the support of seven provinces for the FTA. Seven out of ten would seem to meet the Supreme Court's measure of a "substantial majority" which, in the 1981 Patriation Reference, the Court set down as the level of provincial consent required by Canada's federal political ethic. It is also the degree of consent needed under the patriated constitution for amendments affecting the division of powers. Still, three provinces are opposed to the FTA — Ontario, Manitoba, and Prince Edward Island — and one of these, Manitoba, threatens to launch a court challenge. And so the constitutional question will have to be addressed at the formal level of constitutional law.

What Is the Constitutional Question?

The constitutional question is not whether the agreement signed by Prime Minister Brian Mulroney and President Ronald Reagan in January of 1988 meets the requirements of the Canadian Constitution. The Constitution sets no limits on the agreements or treaties into which the federal government can enter on behalf of Canada with foreign states. Agreements concluded at the executive level do not as such change the internal law of Canada.

Canada's obligation under some international agreements and treaties can be discharged without changing domestic laws — the agreement to test the cruise missile in Canada is an example. But other agreements cannot effectively be carried out without implementing legislation. The Canada-U.S. FTA clearly falls into this category of agreements. At the very least, it calls for changes in Canadian tariff laws. However, only at the stage of legislative implementation — a stage that at the time of writing has not been reached — that a serious constitutional issue arises.

The constitutional question is simply this: Is the legislative power needed to give effect to the FTA within the jurisdiction of the federal Parliament or would some provincial legislation also be needed?

In some federations this question rarely arises. The Australian Constitution, for instance, gives that country's central legislature jurisdiction in the field of "external affairs." This power has been given a wide interpretation by the Australian courts so that the Parliament in Canberra has full powers to pass legislation implementing international agreements on virtually every subject, including subjects that are normally under state jurisdiction.

However, when Canada's Constitution was drawn up this country was, as far as external affairs are concerned, a British colony. The only foreign-affairs jurisdiction the Canadian Constitution explicitly gives the federal Parliament is all powers necessary for performing obligations affecting Canada under British Empire treaties.

When Canada became an autonomous dominion in the 1920s, the federal government entered into international agreements on its own and no longer as part of the British Empire. For a brief moment, in 1932, the Judicial Committee of the Privy Council — until 1949 Canada's highest court — seemed prepared to concede to the federal Parliament the same full, plenary power to pass legislation implementing international agreements entered into by Canada as an independent state as it had to implement British Empire treaties. It viewed this treaty-implementing jurisdiction as falling under Parliament's residual power to legislate for the peace, order, and good government of Canada in matters not exclusively assigned to the provinces.

But five years later the Judicial Committee changed its mind. In the Labour Conventions case it held that "There is no such thing as treaty legislation as such." The essence of this ruling was that the power to implement treaties is subject to the federal division of powers: to the extent that a treaty deals with subjects under exclusive provincial jurisdiction, implementing legislation must be passed by the provincial legislatures. Under this doctrine the key constitutional question is to what extent, if any, does legislation implementing the Canada-U.S. FTA deal with subjects under exclusive provincial jurisdiction?

The Basis of Federal Jurisdiction

It is possible for the Supreme Court of Canada to repudiate the Labour Conventions doctrine and decide that the federal Parliament's jurisdiction to legislate for the peace, order, and good government of Canada includes a plenary power to implement international agreements in all subject matter areas. Since becoming Canada's highest court of appeal in 1949, the Supreme Court is not bound by Privy Council precedents. On a few occasions since 1949 the Court has given some indication of a greater regard for federal authority to carry out Canada's obligations as a sovereign state. Still, it is most unlikely that a majority of the present Court, which has taken a very balanced approach to federal issues, would be willing to go all the way to the highly centralized Australian position and permit Ottawa to take over provincial legislative powers simply by signing foreign treaties.

The much more likely basis for federal jurisdiction is the exclusive federal power to legislate in relation to international trade and commerce. Over the years judicial interpretation cut down the federal Parliament's jurisdiction over "the regulation of trade and commerce" in several respects. But one dimension of trade and commerce that the courts have always included under this head of power is the implementation of international trade agreements. The Judicial Committee referred to these international trade agreements in the 1881 Parsons case, the very first decision on the subject, as "political arrangements in regard to trade requiring the sanction of Parliament."

The modern Supreme Court has shown great concern for maintaining an exclusive federal power to regulate the flow of trade across provincial boundaries. As Chief Justice Kerwin put it in a landmark decision in 1957 (The Ontario Farm

Products Marketing Act Reference): "Once an article enters into the flow of interprovincial or external trade, the subject matter and all its attendant circumstances cease to be a matter of local concern." In the same case, Justice Ivan Rand, recognizing that "trade arrangements reaching the dimensions of world agreements" were becoming "vital to the economic functioning of the country as a whole," said that the "The Dominion power [to regulate trade and commerce] implies responsibility for promoting and maintaining the vigor and growth of trade beyond Provincial confines, and the discharge of this duty must remain unembarrassed by local trade impediments." In 1970, in the Caloil case, the Supreme Court unanimously ruled that federal jurisdiction over international trade extended to controlling where imports could be sold within a province.

At this stage, we can only speculate about what will be in the federal implementing legislation and what form that legislation will take. Certainly not everything in the FTA need be covered in the legislation. Legislation is only needed where changes must be made in the rights and obligations of persons and organizations doing business in or from the Canadian market. It is a fair guess that the federal government will proceed by way of a single act rather than separate bills on different topics. Such an omnibus bill, with all of its provisions clearly tied to performing Canada's obligations under an international trade agreement, clearly has the best chance of passing judicial scrutiny. Even if a few provisions encroached on provincial jurisdiction, they might well be deemed to be "necessarily incidental" to legislation that "in pith and substance" deals with a matter — international trade — under exclusive federal jurisdiction.

It is difficult to envisage any sections of a federal free-trade bill that would not be tied to the international trade aspect of the activity being regulated. Take the sale of wine, for example, a subject over which Ontario's Premier David Peterson seems to think the provinces have exclusive jurisdiction. Now the provinces certainly do have a power to regulate — up to a point — the local sale of virtually any commodity from wine to widgets. But the limit of their power is reached when they legislate so as to regulate the flow of trade into the province. Provinces do not have the power to legislate for the purpose of protecting local producers against foreign competition. I know of no federal nation in the world that gives its constituent units such a power. The question to ask here is actually political not constitutional: Why hasn't the federal government been more vigorous in legislating so as to prevent provinces from discriminating against foreign imports in breach of Canada's obligations under the General Agreement on Tariffs and Trade (GATT)?

The FTA covers much more than has traditionally been dealt with in international trade agreements. Government procurement is covered, but only at the federal level, so there is no possible encroachment on provincial power there. Some services are covered, including many that are regulated by the provinces. But it is most unlikely that the Supreme Court would view the federal power to regulate international trade and commerce as applying only to physical things and not to human services. The FTA's national treatment requirement permits each province to continue to regulate trades and occupations as it sees fit, providing that it does not treat Americans differently from the way it treats out-of-province Canadians. Legislation to ensure this would seem well within federal constitutional powers.

The federal Parliament's exclusive power over "naturalization and aliens" may supplement its trade and commerce power here. If provincial laws restricting foreigners' access to service industries conflict with federal legislation extending national treatment to Americans, the federal jurisdiction should be held to be paramount. The same principle should apply to provincial attempts, such as Premier Howard Pawley of Manitoba is now threatening, to prevent Americans from investing in land. It is true that in the 1976 Morgan case the Supreme Court upheld P.E.I. legislation requiring Cabinet approval for off-islanders' purchases of sea-front properties. That legislation, however, did not focus on aliens but applied to non-islander Canadians as much as to foreigners. Nor did it conflict with any federal legislation concerning the investment rights of aliens. Moreover, in deciding in P.E.I.'s favor, the Supreme Court emphasized the small island province's unique vulnerability to absentee landlordism.

New Provincial Resource Powers

The three resource powers obtained by the provinces in 1982, when a constitutional amendment added Section 92A to the list of provincial powers, might be viewed as the softest spot in the federal government's constitutional armor. These powers apply to non-renewable natural resources, forestry resources, and electrical energy. The first power — exclusive jurisdiction over the exploration, development, and conservation and management of the resources involved — probably creates no serious obstacle to federal implementation of the FTA. The energy provisions simply rule out government-induced price and supply discrimination against U.S. purchasers. It is unlikely that the provincial resource-management power could override exclusive federal jurisdiction over international trade. Nor does the second power — a concurrent jurisdiction over the interprovincial marketing of resources — create a problem.

However, the third of the new provincial resource powers appears to raise a more serious difficulty. This is the power to impose "any mode or system of taxation" on the primary production of the resources concerned "whether or not such production is exported in whole or in part from the province." While the subsection creating this power stipulates that such resource taxes must not discriminate against consumers in other provinces, it is silent on discrimination against foreign customers. The use of this power by one or more of the provinces could collide with the general ban on discriminatory export taxes under chapter 4 of the FTA and possibly with the pricing part of the energy provisions. But this new provincial tax power is not exclusive, so it is reasonable to expect that under the doctrine of federal paramountcy it would have to give way to federal legislation in the field.

Conclusions

The constitutional attack on the proposed free-trade deal with the United States lacks substantial foundation. Even if the fifty-year-old Labour Conventions doctrine were maintained by today's Supreme Court, the legislation needed to give effect to the FTA in Canadian law would seem well within the scope of federal jurisdiction. Provincial advocates have tended to assume that because treaty-implementing legislation must conform to the federal division of powers, no treaty can be implemented without provincial legislation. This is clearly wrong. When the subject matter of a treaty is exclusively or paramountly federal, no provincial legislation is necessary. A treaty dealing with Canada's international trade is under exclusive federal jurisdiction. It is possible that later on, as implementation of the FTA digs deeper into the removal of non-tariff barriers — for instance, establishing and enforcing a subsidies code — further constitutional questions may arise. But here again exclusive federal power over international trade should carry the day.

In consulting with the provinces during the process of negotiating the FTA and in obtaining the support of a substantial majority of the provinces, the federal government went far beyond its formal constitutional obligations. This is entirely appropriate for a country like Canada, which so rigorously adheres to the federal ethic. Despite the weakness of the provincial case there may still be a constitutional challenge. Manitoba is the likely candidate. It could address questions about the federal implementing legislation to the Manitoba Court of Appeal before the legislation is finally enacted or in force. With an appeal to the Supreme Court of Canada, these proceedings might take more than a year to complete.

If this occurs, it is no reason for federal legislators on either side of the border to hold up legislative consummation of the FTA. Certainly U.S. representatives are entirely out of line if they refer to provincial opposition in Canada as a reason for not proceeding. Any such suggestion constitutes an unwarranted and ill-informed intrusion into Canadian affairs. Whatever else can be said about the Canada-U.S. FTA, it can be said to conform with both the letter and the spirit of the Canadian Constitution.

CHAPTER 17
Relationship to the GATT

Concerns have been raised in Canada as well as in the United States that the Canada-U.S. Free-Trade Agreement (FTA) between the two countries will conflict with and weaken the multilateral trade system that has been built during the post-war years around the General Agreement on Tariffs and Trade (GATT). In Canada fears have also been expressed that entering into the FTA with the world's largest economic power will limit Canada's ability to play its traditional leadership role in GATT, and limit Canada's independence in its trade relationships with other countries. These concerns should be taken seriously and deserve continuing analysis and public debate, although they are sometimes put forward by people who have donned the GATT cloak primarily to oppose free trade with the United States.

Canada and the United States have been among the stoutest champions of the GATT since the start. A weakening of support by the two North American countries would have damaging consequences for the multilateral trade system.

This chapter looks into the relationship of the FTA with the GATT, its compatibility with the GATT rules governing

Frank Stone is Senior Research Associate, International Economics Program, Institute for Research on Public Policy, Ottawa. This chapter is an abridged version of a new chapter that will appear in a revised edition of *Canada, the GATT and the International Trade System* by the author, which will be published in the spring of 1988 by the Institute for Research on Public Policy.

free-trade areas, and the freedom of member countries of free-trade areas to participate independently in the GATT and carry on their own independent trade policies and relationships with the rest of the world.

Thirteen years before the GATT came into being in 1935, Canada and the United States concluded a bilateral trade agreement that substantially lowered the excessively high tariffs on bilateral trade that were in place during most of the interwar period. This agreement was suspended in 1948, when the two countries became members of the GATT. Since that time, the GATT has served as Canada's main trade agreement with the United States, as well as the main trade agreement of both countries with most other GATT members. The GATT has provided a body of multilaterally agreed rules that govern the countries' cross-border trade as well as their trade with other countries. It has provided a framework for the progressive reduction of tariffs and other barriers to cross-border trade along with barriers to world trade, and it has provided processes that the two countries have used to resolve a number of bilateral trade disputes as well as their disputes with other GATT members. Outside the GATT, and until the present time, Canada and the United States concluded only a few purely bilateral trade arrangements, notably the auto pact of 1965 that opened up near-free trade in the automotive sector.

The FTA will not replace the GATT as a trade agreement between the two countries, nor can it be viewed as an alternative to the GATT and its supplementary codes. For example, a GATT code will continue to govern the countervailing and anti-dumping systems of the two countries — at least for the next five to seven years while new joint rules governing the use of countervailing and anti-dumping duties are being drawn up. The FTA should be viewed as extending and elaborating the long-standing commitments of the two countries to each other under the GATT.

The FTA will complete the process of cross-border trade liberalization that has been underway under the GATT and on a bilateral basis since the mid-1930s. The removal of tariffs on cross-border trade, which will take place in stages over ten years, would be almost impossible to achieve through the process of multilateral negotiations under the GATT. It would require the removal of Canadian and U.S. tariffs on an most-favored-nation (MFN) basis and this would involve, in effect, the agreement of most other GATT members likewise to remove all of their important tariffs. This is an unlikely prospect in the foreseeable future, although it is to be hoped that existing world tariffs will be lowered substantially as an outcome of the current Uruguay Round of multilateral trade negotiations under the GATT. In this regard, the liberalization achieved by Canada and the United States under the bilateral FTA will set a good example for further trade liberalization on a global scale.

The FTA will reconfirm and extend GATT rules in a number of non-tariff areas between the two countries. It contains special rules, beyond those in the GATT, for the use of safeguard (escape-clause) measures when these are in the GATT, used to limit surges in imports from each other of particular products and also when such measures are imposed on a global basis. The FTA will enlarge the volume of purchases by the two federal governments that will be open to firms in the two countries, beyond the opportunities opened by the GATT code on government procurement. It will go beyond the GATT rules and prohibit the subsidization of cross-border exports of agricultural products. In addition, the FTA clarifies and elaborates the GATT rules that are aimed at the avoidance of product standards that obstruct bilateral trade.

In some other non-tariff areas the GATT rules alone will continue to apply to cross-border trade, as before. These include, as noted above, the GATT rules governing countervailing and anti-dumping duties, at least for the next five to seven years; the use of import restrictions where needed to maintain farm-support programs, and the use of trade measures to protect cultural industries, as well as for the protection of health and public morals, to conserve natural resources, and for national security purposes. Canada's product-labelling requirements are also covered by GATT rules.

The bilateral FTA also covers a number of areas that have not so far been covered by GATT rules, but where GATT rules might well be put in place as an outcome of the Uruguay Round. Some of these elements of the FTA deal with long-standing or potential frictions between the two countries, for example, in regard to controls on foreign investment, cross-border trade in certain services sectors, and trade in energy. The provisions of the bilateral FTA in these sectors could possibly set a useful example and precedent for the negotiations in the Uruguay Round. In some other areas that are excluded from the bilateral FTA, such as the protection of intellectual property, efforts will be made in the Uruguay Round to draw up international rules and disciplines that might then be applied by Canada and the United States to each other.

The GATT rules and procedures for the settlement of trade disputes will remain available to the two countries to deal with bilateral issues, particularly those involving the extensive commitments to each other that will remain under the GATT. But the bilateral FTA also creates its own processes for the resolution of disputes arising from its operation. These processes will include recourse to "binding arbitration" involving the use of independent, joint panels as well as recourse to panels whose findings and recommendations will be advisory in nature. There are separate provisions under the FTA for creating joint panels to carry out "judicial review" of decisions by either country for the use of countervailing and anti-dumping duties, and to review any changes in these systems on either side. These provisions, as noted earlier, will apply over the next five to seven years while new bilateral rules for countervailing and anti-dumping systems are being negotiated.

Consistency of the FTA with the GATT

GATT member countries have always had the right to form free-trade areas and customs unions, provided these correspond to the rules that are set out in GATT Article XXIV, and many such regional trade groups have been formed over the past few decades. The member countries have not needed to seek special permission to form such groups, unless the arrangements have departed in significant ways from the GATT rules. In the latter cases the countries concerned have had to obtain special waivers from their GATT obligations.

No such waivers are expected to be needed for the Canada-U.S. FTA, which appears to be fully compatible with the Article XXIV rules of the GATT that govern the formation and operation of free-trade areas and customs unions. These rules call for the removal of tariffs and export taxes on "substantially all the trade" between members of such trade groups, either immediately or over a reasonable period of time. The FTA will achieve this result over the next ten years. In accordance with GATT rules the FTA will also remove most non-tariff barriers to trade where these exist, with the exception of those that will continue on both sides in fairly large areas of agricultural trade. But, as an exception, the GATT rules permit the continued maintenance of quotas and other restrictions on agricultural products when these are needed to protect supply management and similar farm-support programs. Canada's continued restriction on imports of dairy products, eggs, and poultry are thus in conformity with the rules of the GATT. And although U.S. import restrictions on dairy products, sugar, and some other agricultural products may not be similarly in accord with GATT rules, they are sheltered by a special waiver obtained by the United States in the mid-1950s.

The GATT rules have, in effect, established a large part of the framework within which the FTA, like many other regional trade groups, has been created. The FTA is probably more in line with the GATT rules than most other free-trade areas and customs unions that have been established among GATT member countries. The agreements that established the European Community and the European Free Trade Association, for example, contain features that are widely regarded as inconsistent with GATT, although the New Zealand-Australia and the U.S.-Israel free-trade arrangements have encountered fewer problems in the GATT.

In accordance with established GATT procedures, Canada and the United States have notified the GATT director general of the conclusion of their bilateral agreement. At some early stage, a GATT working group will doubtless be established to examine the FTA in detail. Although it is not expected that the FTA will encounter serious difficulties in Geneva, other GATT members will of course have an opportunity to question its terms and seek to resolve any problems created for their own trade interests. Third-country automotive exporters, for example, might protest the new and more demanding rules of origin that will have to be met for automotive products to qualify for duty-free treatment under the bilateral FTA.

The actual approval of the GATT Contracting Parties is not required for Canada and the United States to proceed to implement the FTA. The European Community, the European Free Trade Association, and most other regional trade groups have neither been approved nor disapproved in Geneva but have nevertheless operated for many years. The GATT Contracting Parties may similarly withhold judgment on the Canada-U.S. FTA, without in any way blocking it. However, they will probably require the submission of periodic reports on its implementation and reserve the right to review its operation.

Members of free-trade agreements, in contrast with members of customs unions, are able to maintain their own independent trade policies and relationships with third countries. They also retain, of course, their separate membership in the GATT. This means that Canada and also the United States will be free to maintain different levels of tariffs and other barriers to trade with third countries. Also, the two countries will be able to negotiate separately in the GATT and elsewhere with third countries to improve access to third-country markets, or to enter into their own, separate arrangements with third countries to achieve their particular objectives.

Canada and the United States will thus participate separately and independently in the Uruguay Round of multilateral trade negotiations. While both governments have stated their intention to play active leadership roles in these negotiations, the goals and objectives of Canada and the United States will not always be in harmony. However, there is nothing in the FTA to prevent Canada from pursuing its own particular negotiating objectives and strategies. The FTA does specifically call for bilateral co-operation in liberalizing and improving the rules governing world agricultural trade. Also, it introduces some new concepts that will be useful in pursuing these common objectives, particularly in regard to the measurement of the trade effects of domestic subsidy programs. This undertaking, however, has not prevented Canada from pursuing objectives for agricultural trade in the Uruguay Round that are rather different from U.S. objectives.

Bilateralism vs. Multilateralism

As noted earlier, the Canada-U.S. FTA is not an alternative to the GATT, but complements and extends the GATT as between the two countries. The GATT will remain as a basic trade agreement between Canada and the United States. The two countries will, of course, extend tariff preferences to each other, and this is an important element of the FTA. Their MFN tariffs, where these apply, will be removed on each other's goods, but their separate tariffs will continue to be imposed on imports subject to duty from other countries, whether on an MFN basis, under special preferential schemes such as those for less-developed countries, or otherwise. Inevitably, exporters in both countries whose goods enjoy free and preferential access in the other market will exert pressure to retain their preferential access and will discourage the reduction of duties that apply on the other side of the border to similar goods from other sources. Canadian exporters may tend to concentrate on the open, preferential U.S. market and overlook broader international markets. In this way, pressures to maintain bilateral and preferential advantages and trade patterns in North America could work against trade liberalization on a global basis, and weaken the multilateral trade system.

However, the FTA will give rise to balancing counter-pressures. Canadian producers of some goods are likely to press for reductions in Canada's tariffs on imports from third countries of machinery, components, and other inputs, in order to reduce their production costs and help them meet increased competition from the United States. Similar pressures could be exerted across the border by U.S. producers for the reduction of U.S. tariffs on their imports of inputs from third countries. Moreover, in both countries consumer groups will doubtless continue to urge reductions in tariffs and other barriers to imports from third countries.

It might also be expected that other countries will be readier than in the past to negotiate reductions in their own tariffs in order to secure reductions in Canadian and U.S. tariffs, and thus reduce adverse effects of the preferential Canada-U.S. FTA on their own export interests. And, in return, Canadian and U.S. policymakers may be more prepared to reduce tariffs against third countries, with the prospect that as a result of the bilateral FTA, their domestic producers will become more competitive and better able to meet global import competition.

On balance, it is difficult at present to make a convincing case that the bilateral FTA will stand in the way of global tariff liberalization. There are precedents, as well as theoretical reasons, for expecting the opposite to happen. Following the formation of regional, preferential groups in Europe, the member countries proceeded in three successive rounds of negotiations in the GATT to bargain substantial reductions in their tariffs against outside countries, including Canada and the United States, at least for non-agricultural products.

As for the non-tariff elements of the FTA, some of these, as noted earlier, may provide useful models and precedents for the negotiation of multilateral arrangements in the areas concerned. This would, of course, require other GATT countries to accept the same kind of rules and disciplines that Canada and the United States have accepted to apply to each other. The experience gained in the Canada-U.S. negotiations of the FTA has doubtless better equipped Canadian and U.S. negotiators to play leadership roles in efforts during the Uruguay Round to develop new or improved rules and arrangements on a global basis in a range of non-tariff areas. There is no evidence to date that the FTA has changed or undermined the positive approaches and positions of either government toward strengthening and improving the GATT system.

The FTA could well lead to a strengthening of the GATT system rather than work against it. The liberalization of trade in North America on a preferential basis could provide new incentives for dismantling trade barriers on a global basis. Over the past several decades a vast preferential, tariff-free commercial system has grown up in western Europe surrounding the European Community. On both sides of the Atlantic, pressures could now emerge for the elimination or reduction of trade preferences, and the current Uruguay Round of multilateral trade negotiations offers a framework to initiate such a process, as well as to pursue broader efforts to liberalize trade in goods and services on a global basis. Optimistically, the eventual outcome could be the complete removal of tariffs and many other barriers to trade, at least by the developed countries for industrial products.

Conclusions

The Canada-United States FTA will complement but will not

replace the GATT, and GATT rules will continue to govern important areas of bilateral trade as in the past. The FTA conforms to the GATT rules that govern the formation and operation of free-trade areas, and is not likely to give rise to serious objections by other GATT member countries, although these countries can be expected to raise problems that may be created for their own particular trade interests.

Canada, as well as the United States, will continue to maintain its own separate and distinct trade policies and relationships with third countries, as well as its independent membership in the GATT. Both countries can be expected to play active leadership roles in the Uruguay Round of multilateral trade negotiations under the GATT, where the objectives of the two countries may well differ. The FTA could set useful examples and precedents for global trade liberalization and for the strengthening of the GATT system, and it could provide new incentives for efforts during the Uruguay Round to reduce preferences within the world trade system and remove tariffs and other barriers on a global basis.

The Canada-U.S. FTA could thus, on balance, create pressures to strengthen the GATT system, and not to weaken it. There is no evidence to date that the FTA has changed or weakened the positive approaches and positions of either country toward enlarging, improving, and strengthening the GATT system.

CHAPTER 18
A U.S. Perspective

"Historic" is the most appropriate word to describe the agreement signed on January 2, 1988, by the United States and Canada, creating a free-trade area between the world's largest trading partners. The two countries have flirted with the idea of some type of special trading arrangement for more than a century. But on almost every occasion, one side or the other has backed out. This time both countries saw the negotiations to their conclusion. Although the Canada-U.S. Free-Trade Agreement (FTA) still needs to be implemented, the mere fact that it was negotiated will have a profound effect on the world trading system. Even if the FTA is not implemented, the history of U.S. and Canadian trade policy will have been altered by these negotiations. The status quo that existed before the talks will no longer prevail.

What was different this time? How will the FTA affect the world trading system now and in the future? Does the FTA represent a turning point in U.S. trade policy? What would happen if it were not implemented?

The negotiation of a bilateral agreement with Canada (and earlier with Israel) came amid a period of widespread uncer-

C. Michael Aho is Director of Economic Studies and Director of the International Trade Project, Council on Foreign Relations, Inc., New York City. The Council on Foreign Relations' International Trade Project is a multiyear project designed to contribute to the public policy debate on trade policy issues. A series of ten to twelve monographs will be produced over the next two years. Two that have appeared to date, *Trade Talks: America Better Listen!* and *Bilateralism, Multilateralism and Canada in U.S. Trade Policy*, relate directly to the FTA.

tainty over the future course of U.S. trade policy. The willingness to pursue bilateral negotiations was just one way in
which U.S. trade policy fundamentally changed under the
Reagan Administration. Unprecedented deficits, unprecedented neglect of Congress, and unprecedented private sector complaints spawned unprecedented administrative and
legislative action on trade.

In late 1985 after almost five years of neglect of trade
issues, the Reagan Administration declared that the high dollar was not a sign of strength but the source of trade problems, self-initiated over a dozen unfairness complaints
against other countries, and set the bilateral negotiations with
Canada in motion. Since then sanctions have been applied
against Japan, and according to Treasury Secretary James
Baker, the Reagan Administration has provided more import
relief than any of its predecessors in the past fifty years.

Meanwhile, Congress was threatening to pass restrictive
trade measures. In 1985 alone, three hundred protectionist
bills were introduced in the Congress. In 1987, both
chambers of Congress passed trade bills unprecedented in
size and in scope. Both bills exceed one thousand pages. (The
Reciprocal Trade Agreements Act of 1934, the most important U.S. trade legislation, was only three pages long.) The
bills were drafted by more than twenty Congressional committees, and in addition to traditional trade-remedy legislation, they cover everything from plant-closing notification to
developing country debt. A conference committee composed of a record 199 members of Congress plans to report
out a compromise bill this spring before Congress turns its
attention to the Canada-U.S. FTA. The Administration is
struggling to minimize the extent to which that legislation
will make it easier to obtain import relief and reduce presidential flexibility in resolving trade disputes. Needless to say,
the United States was and is struggling to find its way on
trade policy — and the world is waiting nervously.

Against this dark backdrop, the Reagan Administration
deserves credit for successfully negotiating the FTA with

Canada, because it did signal that trade liberalization is still possible and that international negotiations can still bear fruit. But it did come perilously close to failure. Frustrated by lack of progress on the multilateral front, the United States in effect backed into the bilateral negotiations with Canada. Throughout most of the negotiations the Administration appeared not to appreciate the significance of the bilateral talks. Consultations with Congress and the private sector were spotty and the Administration did not take sufficient steps to mobilize allies in the legislature. In the closing weeks, Treasury Secretary Baker was brought in to provide political impetus and to close the deal, but even then it was not completed until six minutes before the deadline.

Now both sides must make sure that the FTA is implemented. In the United States the outlook for implementation is good provided that the Administration — in conjunction with the private sector — initiates a broad-scale educational effort on Capitol Hill as to the benefits of an agreement and successfully negotiates an omnibus trade bill that the U.S. president can sign. Fortunately, the Administration and the private sector now realize that failure to implement the FTA could mark an unfortunate turning point in U.S. trade policy.

The bilateral talks coincided with the launching of the Uruguay Round of multilateral trade negotiations under the auspices of the General Agreement on Tariffs and Trade (GATT). The simultaneity of the bilateral and multilateral negotiations means that, on the one hand, a successful bilateral could be a catalyst for the multinational, but on the other hand, a failure of the bilateral talks would send a very bad signal to the rest of the world and the Uruguay Round would suffer a setback. If the United States and Canada cannot implement an agreement in the new issue areas of services and investment, how much can be expected in a multinational forum where the common denominator is much lower?

The Reagan Administration would have sacrificed its only opportunity to demonstrate the benefits of a liberalizing strategy to a restive Congress. Without a bilateral or a credible multilateral option, Congress will be more likely to act unilaterally.

But enough of the negative. What positive factors resulted from the FTA negotiations? Without a doubt, these negotiations have provided a valuable learning experience for both countries. Most of the issues being negotiated in Geneva are the same as those negotiated in the bilateral FTA. You learn to negotiate by negotiating, and both countries learned a great deal. You learn the pitfalls, the problems, the stumbling blocks, as you go through the negotiating process. And when tentative deals are brought back to show to the domestic constituencies that must be co-opted, these constituencies also learn from the process. In this manner the tradeoffs are explored, the political sentiments are assessed, and political leaders are forced to confront tough choices.

For years the U.S. Congress has been talking about the need for greater discipline in subsidies and for rules covering services, investment, and intellectual property, but no one ever asked the U.S. Congress to do anything or to give anything in exchange for greater discipline or new rules. The tradeoffs were largely unexplored, but during the final weeks of the FTA negotiation the U.S. Congress became more aware of these tradeoffs as they were consulted more frequently. The U.S. private sector also learned a great deal in the process. They learned that the area of services contains heterogeneous sectors and they learned about the pitfalls and stumbling blocks in some of those sectors, such as shipping. They learned that services is not just a collection of sectors in which the United States has a competitive advantage. Now both countries' negotiators can take these lessons to the negotiations in Geneva.

The tariff-cutting and trade-liberalizing measures mean, of course, that both countries will be richer in the long run. But more important from a U.S. perspective these bilateral talks resulted in pioneering, path-breaking agreements that could serve as a catalyst for the Uruguay Round. Canada and the United States have gone farther and faster in services and investment than they could reasonably expect to achieve in the multilateral talks, and if these agreements are tabled in Geneva that could accelerate that process.

The FTA could have a valuable demonstration effect on the U.S. Congress, where the perception is that the U.S. government has always sold itself out in international trade negotiations. The Congress is looking for a way to solve problems, but they believe problems cannot be solved through international negotiations because they lack credibility — they never yield anything substantial. But just maybe the FTA has provided some solutions and something substantial has been achieved. The way we will know that is if the private sector in the United States and in Canada comes forward and vocally proclaims, "This is what we have always wanted. This is something concrete." The U.S. private sector will be the ultimate judge of the FTA. If they believe the agreement is a good one and they speak up and tell their elected representatives, it will have a salutary effect on the trade-policy process in the United States, and it will improve the prospects for the Uruguay Round.

Trade policymaking is a delicate balancing act, even in the best of times. It always pays for the import-competing interests to complain and to ask for government help and protection. Under normal circumstances, a countervailing force of exporters and those interests with a stake in open market can be mobilized to tell the other side of the story. But the last seven years have been anything but normal in the United States. U.S. exports in 1986 were less than in 1980. When exports are flat or declining, legislators cannot count on hearing from that countervailing force to balance against the complaining interests. Congress has been hearing only one side of the story. So if the private sector speaks up and begins to tell the other side of the story, trade policymaking in the United States will be improved and the Uruguay Round will have more credibility. Fortunately, we are beginning to see signs that the services sectors and some of the larger foreign investors are mobilizing in order to "sell" the FTA to Congress.

The Uruguay Round will be different, more difficult, and probably will last longer than any of the seven rounds that preceded it. It could take ten years but the U.S. Congress will not wait that long for results. Here again, a successful implementation of the FTA could enhance the prospects of the Uruguay Round. To the extent that the agreements in these new areas break new ground, they could help to shorten the duration of the Round and bring it to a successful conclusion before the U.S. Congress loses its patience.

The binding nature of dispute settlement in the FTA could also set a precedent for similar action on a multilateral basis. The dispute-settlement provisions will provide an external discipline on both countries. Both countries have arbitrarily changed or capriciously applied their laws that govern foreign commerce. In response to political pressure, the United States has been known to apply its trade-remedy laws in inconsistent ways to the detriment of both foreign and domestic interests. For its part, Canada has arbitrarily changed its laws governing foreign investors also to the detriment of foreign and domestic interests. The FTA — an international obligation on the part of both countries — should help to avoid such situations in the future. After all what is the true value of international obligations? International obligations are what a government can use to protect itself against its own worse instincts.

And what of the future? How durable will the FTA be? An agreement such as this creates a whole host of legal, political, and institutional questions. Ideally, you want an agreement that is strong enough to hold together over time and yet flexible enough to evolve with changing circumstances.

The FTA is not an ideal agreement by any stretch of the imagination. The failure to develop a common set of rules to govern subsidies and to reach an agreement on intellectual property protection are two of the more obvious drawbacks from a U.S. perspective. But it is a good agreement, and we should not allow the best to be the enemy of the good. Our task is to make the good better and to fill in the deficiencies over time. With good faith on both sides, I am confident that the institutional and administrative apparatus created under the FTA will provide a mechanism to fill in the gaps.

Concern has been expressed that the FTA is a step toward a breakdown and a fragmentation of the trading system. Some in Canada wonder if the United States will continue to sign bilateral agreements that will disadvantage Canada and will result in the fragmentation of the trading system. President Reagan in his 1988 State of the Union address spoke of including Mexico in a North American accord. Mexico is the most obvious possible other bilateral agreement, and I am certain Canada would want to have something to say about it. But let me hasten to add that neither the United States nor Mexico is likely to sign a significant trade-liberalizing agreement in the near future. Mexican firms are fearful of being overrun by American firms and Mexican nationalists have always portrayed the United States in the most unflattering manner. For their part, U.S. labor unions would not want to compete with lower-priced Mexican labor.

Frankly, I believe that the bilateral trend (as far as bilateral free-trade agreements are concerned) in U.S. trade policy is limited. Israel and Canada are special cases. Mexico may also be a special case, but after that it is hard to see the U.S. Congress and the private sector in the United States going along with any other bilateral free-trade agreements. Policymakers in the United States realize that a succession of bilaterals is a recipe for RIBS — resentment, inefficiency, bureaucracy, and stupid signals. Resentment would prevail among outsiders. Inefficiency would be spawned by the fragmentation of markets. Bureaucratic nightmares would result for the government and private firms trying to cope with the discrimination among countries. And stupid signals would be sent to those policymakers in developing countries who are proponents of markets and multilateralism. Lastly, other countries would protest if the United States tried to go beyond these special cases. After Canada, Israel, and maybe Mexico some time in the next century, the options are spent.

How will progress or lack thereof at the Uruguay Round affect the agreement? During the bilateral talks, both countries were constrained by the multilateral talks. For example, the United States did not want to go too far on agriculture. Its major complaints are against the European Community. If the United States and Canada were fundamentally to change their farm programs as part of the bilateral agreement, then they both would have fewer bargaining chips and less leverage in the Uruguay Round.

But what happens if contentious issues like agriculture do not get resolved in the Uruguay Round? Perhaps what we need is a sequential negotiating process by which Canada and the United States agree to recontract after the multilateral talks are completed in order to improve the bilateral FTA. That would enhance the durability of the FTA.

Finally, a question often posed by Canadian friends: Will the United States hold up its side of the bargain? Yes, if the completed FTA is the result of an active, vocal private sector "selling" it to Congress, explaining that the FTA is in their commercial interest. On completion of the FTA they are going to respond to its provisions by investing, planning their sourcing and operations, and redirecting resources. Although the private sector is not homogeneous, those parts that change their behavior will have a vested interest in the FTA's integrity. If someone proposes abrogating or undermining the FTA they will mobilize in opposition and that will increase the likelihood that the United States will stick to its side of the bargain. I hope and trust that the Canadian private sector would do likewise. After all, true interests do cut across national borders.

All in all, how should the FTA be rated? On balance, the FTA is a plus — not a big plus, but that is substantially better than the big minus that would have resulted if the two countries could not reach an agreement.

Conclusion

The articles in this book speak for themselves. Given half a chance, so does the Canada-U.S. Free-Trade Agreement (FTA). The problem is that few Canadians are taking the trouble to find out for themselves what this historic agreement is all about. Instead many are allowing themselves to be deceived and misled by those who are determined to scuttle the FTA, regardless of its merits.

A Loaded and Stacked Debate

Rather than reviewing and summarizing each of the foregoing chapters, this concluding section will concentrate on the misconceptions that naturally exist and the misrepresentations that have been spread about the FTA. Distorted and misleading accounts of the contents of the FTA have gained far more credence than they deserve, due to the highly emotional nature of much of the attack on the FTA. This has been aided and abetted by powerful nationalistic elements within the media.

Many of the critics and opponents of free trade have charged that the FTA represents a sellout of basic Canadian interests and will turn Canada into the fifty-first U.S. state. As this book has proven, these charges are not supported by the facts about the FTA.

A well-known academic has said that the FTA will generate more crime and drugs on Canadian streets. A celebrated author has said that the FTA will result in the pillage and rape of Canada. One politician has even suggested that it will lead to more surrogate motherhood in this country. A publisher has claimed that the FTA will force Canada to accept nuclear weapons on its soil and to participate in the U.S. Star Wars program. All of these charges represent ridiculous commentary.

Other ill-informed critics and opponents of the FTA claim that it will take away Canadians' jobs — particularly from women — and their culture, medical plans, and pensions, not to mention their sovereignty, if not their very existence. The truth about the FTA obviously counts for absolutely nothing in many quarters.

The anti-FTA exponents are allowed to exploit their alarmist warnings to the fullest because of their network of sympathizers in the media. It would appear that the FTA has no hope of receiving a fair review from many media representatives. Many people are thus being turned against an economic treaty that could be instrumental in shaping a better future for all Canadians.

The most appalling example of this lack of journalistic integrity is embodied by *The Toronto Star*. Unlike *The Globe and Mail*, which editorially favors the FTA but features almost 40% anti-free-trade commentaries on its op-ed page, *The Toronto Star* was at one point running more than 90% anti-free-trade material in its unrelenting campaign against the agreement. And it was doing this in the critical southern Ontario market — which it dominates — where, partially as a result of the *Star*'s role, there is more fear and suspicion of the FTA than in any other part of Canada.

Far more unforgivable is the similar approach being pursued by the Canadian Broadcasting Corporation in its national radio and television programming. As a publicly owned broadcasting system, the CBC has an obligation to be more balanced and fair in its coverage than any other media outlet. Yet the CBC plays up anti-free-trade stories while playing down anything running the other way.

A typical example of this deliberate strategy was evidenced by the CBC program *National*'s handling of the reaction by the Council of Canadians and by the Canadian Alliance for Trade and Job Opportunities to the final version of the FTA. The Council's negative reaction was the second item on the *National*, with no contrary flak running either before or after it. In contrast, the Alliance's subsequent positive reaction was the fifth item on the *National* and was preceded by an item featuring a distorted account of the purported job loss due to free trade and followed by an undistorted account of the legitimate fears of Okanagan fruit and vegetable farmers after their twenty-year seasonal protection expires.

The media in general revealed themselves at their worst during the House of Commons committee hearings on free trade. Whenever the critics of free trade appeared, the media showed up in droves and duly reported the critic's opinions, with particular emphasis on the more sensational of these. Then when the proponents of free trade appeared, the media virtually abandoned the hearings and reported little or nothing of their more factual presentations. There was a deliberate, unmistakable pattern to this totally unprofessional treatment of the two sides of this critical national debate before the committee.

The Debate Revolving Around the Agreement

Turning to the misconceptions and misrepresentations about free trade it is useful to begin with those surrounding the negotiation of the FTA. Only five of the most glaring of these will be dealt with here. These five cover the real choice confronting Canada in its trading relations with the United States, the real lack of any meaningful short-term alternative, the real basis of support for free trade, the real basis for much of the opposition to it, and the real costs of a failure to achieve an agreement.

With the help of the media the opponents of free trade continue to strive to create the impression that the real alternative to free trade with the United States is the status quo. The truth is, of course, that there is no such thing as the status quo. In fact, as was indicated in the Introduction of this book, the real choice is between free trade and growing U.S.

protectionism, as exemplified by the various versions of the infamous omnibus trade bill, the growing support for gutting the auto pact, and the hundreds of industry-specific protectionist bills circulating the halls of the U.S. Congress.

Without free trade any major protectionist thrust in the United States could prove very serious for Canada. As deserves to be repeated frequently, this is because Canada now relies on the U.S. market for nearly 80% of its exports and these exports alone account for about 25% of Canada's gross national product. There is no escaping from these economic realities, because Canada has been too high cost a producer of most products and services to compete successfully other than in the United States. Undoubtedly, this situation will change under the FTA as more Canadian producers learn to compete in the larger U.S. market and subsequently in even more competitive offshore markets.

The opponents of free trade are also very misleading about any real alternative to the FTA. Again, as was stressed in the Introduction, most of them fall back on the General Agreement on Tariffs and Trade (GATT) alternative. However, many of them have even become a little squeamish about it since the GATT ruled against Canada in two recent trade disputes. The FTA complements and is consistent with the GATT — a vital point that is repeatedly reflected in the many cross-references in the FTA to the GATT and its supplementary codes. Both Canada and the United States are committed to a dual track of bilateral and multilateral free trade as the most effective twin ways of reducing trade barriers between both each other and the rest of the world.

As was discussed earlier the problem with relying on the GATT alone is twofold. In the first place the GATT is on a four- to five-year negotiating timetable. This is too long for Canada to wait in the face of rising protectionist pressures within its major trading partner to the south. Moreover a GATT breakthrough is anything but a sure thing. Quite appropriately the United States is demanding that other countries reduce their agricultural and service trade barriers.

The United States is simply unwilling to continue to accept higher trade barriers where it has a comparative trade advantage, while maintaining lower trade barriers where it is at a comparative disadvantage.

Even if there is a GATT breakthrough, Canada would be wise to be well along the way to full implementation of the FTA, since this would give Canadian firms a chance to build to the scale and volume they require to be world-class competitors. Conversely, Canada would by then be able to begin the transfer of workers to more viable industries from its low-paid, highly protected and subsidized industries, which are much more vulnerable to offshore than U.S. competition.

Perhaps those who are fighting the FTA are most dishonest about the nature of the real forces for and against free trade. For shrewd political reasons the opponents of free trade like to pretend that the only major support for it comes from big business, particularly the Business Council on National Issues. If you want to do a smear job on this vital initiative, it is good politics to associate free trade with this group of leaders of Canada's largest corporations, because it is not the most popular group in the country.

What the opponents of the FTA do not care to acknowledge is that free trade is also supported by consumers, as represented by the Consumers' Association of Canada, and small business, as represented by the Canadian Federation of Independent Business. Least of all do they want to mention the position of the Canadian Manufacturers Association, which played a key role in defeating the 1911 free-trade initiative but now strongly supports the FTA.

The opponents of the FTA are also less than honest about the basis of much of their own opposition. It would be so refreshing if those who oppose the FTA for essentially ideological, philosophical, and political reasons would be frank enough to say so. After all there is nothing wrong with opposing free trade because you are a socialist and you want to socialize Canada, and you think that this will be more difficult to accomplish if this country has closer economic ties with the one country in the world that remains most committed to a competitive enterprise market system.

Opposition to the FTA has been led by organized labor and the New Democratic Party. They lump free trade, privatization, and deregulation together, opposing them all both in principle and practice. There is every reason why they should do so since the last thing they wish to contemplate is anything that commits this country to less government intervention. It is extremely misleading but readily understandable why they are so unwilling to state the underlying socialist basis for their opposition to the FTA, since it clearly would not appeal to the majority of the Canadian public.

Finally, the opponents of free trade are being anything but candid about the costs of failing to consummate a free-trade agreement with the United States. Already cited has been the threat of the omnibus trade bill and the potential gutting of the auto pact. Two other probable serious consequences merit attention. The first relates to the exciting and growing number of Canadian entrepreneurs who have found a special market niche that they are exploiting on both sides of the border.

Without free trade many of these entrepreneurs will have to establish branch plants in the United States to ensure access to that huge market, a process that has already begun but could become a tidal wave. Before long those plants will be their main plants and eventually it will be a question of whether they maintain any meaningful Canadian operation at all.

The right kind of foreign investment in Canada will also be jeopardized by failure to achieve free trade. Generally speaking, except in a narrow band of resource industries, it does not make sense to invest in Canada unless one has ready access to the U.S. market. This is because in most industries the Canadian market is too small to support a viable modern operation. Some tariff-jumping, branch-plant, foreign investment would doubtless continue in Canada but it would remain inefficient and threatened by any kind of trade liberalization.

The Debate about the FTA Itself

At least six major misconceptions and misrepresentations are also being promulgated about the FTA itself. The grossest of these misconceptions and misrepresentations revolve around those provisions of the deal relating to dispute settlement, the auto pact, energy, investment, services, and directly and indirectly, Canada's sovereignty. All of these misconceptions and misrepresentations have been dealt with earlier in this book but their rebuttal merits repetition here.

On the dispute-settlement front the opponents of the FTA are disparaging and maligning what was accomplished by claiming that all that Canada achieved was the right to challenge U.S. decisions under U.S. laws, albeit before a binding binational dispute-settlement panel. This falls short of the code of fair trade behavior and related dispute-settlement machinery that Canada and the United States are committed to negotiate during the first five to seven years of the FTA. Nevertheless, it is very important to Canada in the interim for two sets of reasons.

The first of these reasons relates to the view that U.S. laws in relation to countervail and anti-dumping cases have not been the problem in and of themselves. Instead the problem has arisen from the unfair administration and interpretation of these U.S. laws over the last half-dozen years. An example of this transformation is the softwood-lumber case, which Canada won on essentially the same evidence only three years before it lost it. In the interval the United States drifted away from a basically economic approach toward a more political one in its countervail and anti-dumping decisions.

Under the free-trade dispute-settlement mechanism, Canada has the means to "objectify" once again the U.S. decision-making process in these types of cases. This is because Canada will be able to take the final appeal on these cases to the binding binational tribunal established under the FTA. Moreover, the basis of any such appeal will be the administrative record in the cases involved, which includes all the evidence, information, and even hearsay introduced in the earlier proceedings in which Canadian representatives fully participate.

Had Canada been able to appeal the softwood-lumber case under such a system — especially to a binding binational panel — the decision probably would have been reversed. Having the ability to appeal to such a body in the future will avoid other similar cases, compel the applicable U.S. tribunals to be more objective in their future deliberations, and thus, in all likelihood, eliminate all manner of capricious and frivolous cases from ever coming forward in the first place.

The second reason why the FTA is critical to Canada in the countervail and anti-dumping disputes arena relates to possible changes in U.S. laws in these areas. There is always the risk of these laws themselves becoming even more of a hurdle in the future because of congressional action.

Consequently, great emphasis must be placed on the "legislative watchdog" component of the FTA, which ensures a standstill on new countervail and anti-dumping laws unless a number of stringent tests are met by the country that wants to introduce such changes. By making such changes more difficult to introduce, Canadian producers will be able to export into the United States with much more certainty about what is likely or unlikely to give rise to a countervail or anti-dumping challenge.

No greater misconceptions prevail about the FTA than those relating to the auto industry. There has been a growing alliance of U.S. pressure groups calling for a gutting of the auto pact, including the removal of the Canadian production safeguards. This alliance includes the seven governors and seven congressional delegations of the seven leading automobile-producing states, as well as the United Automobile

Workers, which no longer has any vested interests in Canada since the decision to take the Canadian members out of that great international union.

Under the FTA the auto pact has not been gutted. Far from it. The two principal Canadian safeguards — one the assembly ratio and the other the Canadian value-added provision — have both been preserved. Although the gradual removal of all auto and auto-parts tariffs between the two countries eliminates one of the incentives for complying with these safeguards, another very important one remains. That is the related right of the Big-Three auto makers to import offshore autos and parts duty free, which they currently do to the tune of about $3 billion a year.

In addition, the 50% North American-content rule (which applies to offshore manufacturers who choose to establish production facilities in Canada and the United States and to transfer finished cars duty-free between the two countries) has been refined to make it a much more stringent requirement. This is an important new incentive for auto-parts producers on both sides of the border.

The energy provisions in the FTA have proven very controversial because they are so poorly understood, particularly in relation to other international commitments Canada has already undertaken in the energy sphere. On the plus side Canada has been guaranteed virtually free access to the United States for its electricity, gas, oil, and uranium exports. The importance of this access is not to be minimized, since assured markets for such exports are essential to generate the funding required to finance the megaprojects necessary to exploit these energy supplies. A share of the production of some of these megaprojects is essential to Canada's own energy security.

In return for relatively free access to the U.S. market for these energy supplies, Canada has made two concessions that are probably inevitable if it wants to secure long-term sales commitments in the United States. In the first place, it has guaranteed that it will not resort to government measures to extract more from U.S. customers for these energy sources than it does from their Canadian counterparts. It is to be stressed that this does not mean that Canadian suppliers — private or public — cannot charge their U.S. customers more than they do their Canadian counterparts. It only means that Canadian governments cannot induce such an effort through export taxes or the like.

Canada has also assured the United States that in time of crisis it will not cut back on energy exports to the United States more than proportionately to the cutbacks that it imposes within Canada. Two points are to be stressed about this commitment. First, it is to be emphasized that Canada is under no compulsion to sell any energy to the United States. Only the amount that it does choose to sell is subject to proportionate cutbacks in a crunch situation, and then only for the duration of existing contractual arrangements. Second, Canada is already legally committed to such proportionate cutbacks, both for oil under the 1976 International Energy Agency and for all forms of energy under the GATT.

The investment component of the FTA is another sensitive topic, again in part because of uncalled-for misapprehension about what was negotiated. In return for national treatment of Canadian investment in the United States — an important concession given growing U.S. sensitivity to foreign investment — Canada has agreed to raise its threshold for reviewing U.S. takeovers of Canadian firms from $5 million to $150 million. Although this may seem to be too much of a jump, it still leaves approximately five hundred Canadian firms, representing roughly two-thirds of corporate assets in this country, subject to review in the event of a takeover. It should also be emphasized that the $5-million takeover threshold remains in effect in the cultural, energy, and mining industries, while non-national ownership restrictions have been grandfathered in a host of other industries.

The services component of the FTA has also led to a lot of confusion, particularly in relation to the provision of such sensitive services as day-care and health care. What is most galling about the misgivings that the critics of the FTA have been stirring up in the latter cases is that day-care and most health services are not covered by the FTA and therefore can be regulated in any way Canada sees fit, including in a discriminatory fashion. Canada can also regulate all other services covered by the FTA but only in a non-discriminatory fashion, granting national treatment to U.S. providers of such services.

Canada's Sovereignty and Survival as a National Entity

Since any agreement between independent countries involves some compromise of their respective sovereign powers, the only question worth raising is whether the degrees of compromise involved were worth the mutual advantages derived by the FTA. From a Canadian point of view there is no doubt that the country yielded some sovereignty in relation to the energy, investment, and services sectors. On the other hand it can be argued that Canada gained in its sovereignty vis-à-vis the United States through the dispute-settlement mechanism that is incorporated into the FTA.

To date in countervail and anti-dumping cases, Canada has been appearing as little more than a supplicant before U.S. tribunals, where it has had voice but not vote. Instead of this degrading and demeaning situation, Canada will appear as an equal partner under the FTA before a binding bilateral panel where it has equal voice and vote. In terms of its status or sovereignty relative to that of the United States, this change will make Canada the envy of the world.

At this point some attention must also be devoted to the FTA's purported threat to Canada's very existence. As this argument goes it is alleged that a free-trade agreement between Canada and the United States must lead inexorably through a customs union, common market, and economic union to political absorption and the disappearance of Canada as a separate national entity. Despite the lack of any meaningful recent historical precedents in keeping with this thesis, it persists among those who will resort to any length to defeat the FTA.

In fact, an equally if not more cogent argument can be mounted to oppose this thesis. It is quite conceivable that the failure to secure a free-trade agreement with the United States could lead Canada to disintegrate and fall piece by piece into its neighbor to the south. If the Canada-U.S. FTA is not implemented and the United States becomes more and more protectionist, Canada could suffer severe economic consequences.

Assuming that this situation was not easily rectified — and it would *not* be easy to remedy — Canada's standard of living could start to fall relative to that of the United States. At some point — probably starting in the western provinces — this would lead Canadians in various parts of the country to wonder about the price of being Canadian. While it may now be worth 20% less to be a Canadian, it might not be deemed so worthwhile at 25%, 30%, or 35% less. One does not have to be a doctrinaire economic determinist to draw the conclusion that at some point the majority of Canadians might well decide it would be better to join the United States than suffer any further decline in their comparative standard of living.

Adjustments and Adjustment Assistance

As some of the earlier chapters have revealed, free trade will obviously require some adjustments in Canada. Most multinational corporations, whether domestic or foreign-based, appear well positioned to accommodate fairly readily to free trade. At the other extreme, some purely Canadian companies are so inefficient that they will find it more difficult to do so and a few will probably go under. These companies probably could not survive any realistic outward-looking trade strategy for Canada and would be even more vulnerable in the face of a GATT breakthrough.

While some government assistance, particularly in marketing, may well be appropriate for smaller firms trying to penetrate the U.S. market, it is doubtful whether this assistance should go beyond the sponsorship of trade missions and shows and the like. It is all too easy for more generous forms of such support to begin as a temporary kind of infant-industry program but then degenerate into quasi-permanent if not permanent subsidies.

The employment effects of free trade and particularly the impact on women have been exaggerated but are nevertheless real. However, the employment shifts required to move workers, female or male, from losing to winning industries under free trade are far from unmanageable, particularly in relation to the much larger shifts that are taking place in the labor force because of a host of other ongoing changes in the economy.

Although existing manpower-adjustment programs are probably capable of carrying much of the burden of the labor market shifts that will be caused by free trade, additional funding may be required. As the need arises, such funding should be made available for retraining, upgrading, relocation, and income-maintenance programs for those workers willing to help themselves under such programs. Otherwise a disproportionate share of the cost will be borne by the few who must bear the brunt of the adjustments required to meet the free-trade challenge.

Other Vital Concerns

The constitutional issues surrounding free trade will doubtless be debated until the Supreme Court has a chance to rule on them. Although no one should try to second-guess the Supreme Court, there is good reason to believe that it will uphold the right of the federal government to enter into such an agreement under its foreign affairs and trade and commerce powers, even though there may be ancillary effects on provincial powers. Otherwise Canada will not be able to act effectively as a single entity in any of the range of economic relations it has to maintain with foreign powers and international institutions.

Before turning to the reasons why the United States should ratify the FTA, it is critical to refute the argument that it is foolish for Canada to enter into any such agreement with an alleged falling economic star. While the United States is going through a period of severe economic adjustment — largely due to the repercussions of its massive federal government deficits — it is erroneous to assume that the country is heading into a long period of secular decline.

There are two major reasons for disputing this view. In the first place, the United States is still recognized as one of the safest havens for investment capital in the world. In the second place, the fall in the value of the U.S. dollar is making the United States competitive again in a host of areas where it has recently been in great difficulty. The fact that the United States is starting to export both automobiles and steel to Japan is proof of this turnaround.

Even if one assumes that the United States is not going to expand the way it has in the past, it will remain the world's largest and wealthiest single market for years to come. Canada cannot lose by achieving more ready and secure access to that market for the foreseeable future.

The United States should ratify the FTA on economic grounds alone, even if the history of such agreements is that the smaller partner invariably gains more than the larger partner. Despite this normal differential, the United States has done well by the FTA, particularly by establishing a highly desirable international precedent in terms of the agricultural, investment, and services sectors.

The United States should also consider other geopolitical ramifications of the FTA aside from the excellent example it provides for the GATT. It should contemplate the consequences for Canada and therefore for Canadian-U.S. relations if it does not ratify the FTA and continues down a protectionist path.

The first thing the United States should appreciate is the

real significance of Canada's trade surplus with it. This trade surplus, or deficit from the U.S. point of view, bothers many people in the United States although it should not, because Canada needs it to pay the interest and dividends on its accumulated U.S.-held bonds and shares as well as to finance its huge tourist deficit with the United States. If the United States wants to risk those interest and dividend payments and to jeopardize a good share of its tourist revenue in a few key states, then it *should* cut Canada off in terms of trade.

The second effect of not ratifying the FTA could be even more traumatic from a U.S. point of view, since it might have a very deleterious impact on Canada's economy and consequently on the political balance of power in this country. The worst-case scenario of U.S. protectionism could cause irreparable harm to Canada's economy and lead to a dramatic shift to the political left.

Aside from their general government interventionist proclivities, both the far left wing of the Liberal Party and the New Democratic Party are dubious, to say the least, about the North Atlantic Treaty Organization (NATO) and the North American Aerospace Defence Command (NORAD). If these are the political elements that the United States wants to see strengthened in Canada, it could probably do so by rejecting free trade with Canada and turning in a more protectionist direction vis-à-vis this country.

If the United States is wise enough to ratify the FTA, it must ensure that there is no fundamental incompatibility between the FTA and the U.S. omnibus trade bill, in whatever form this bill emerges from the administrative and congressional mills. There is no way that Canada can live with the FTA in the event of any such basic inconsistency.

A Final Assessment

The Canada-U.S. FTA clearly could not and obviously did not yield Canada everything it wanted. It is quite naturally the net result of a complex series of tradeoffs that could not possibly satisfy everyone on either side, let alone both sides of the border. It is a comprehensive but not complete free-trade deal because some exceptions remain — some at Canada's request and others at the request of the United States.

There is no general code of fair-trade behavior that sorts out acceptable and unacceptable subsidization practices in the two countries, although there is a commitment to work out such a code during the first five to seven years of the FTA. There is only the beginning of a general government procurement policy, ensuring national treatment of suppliers in both countries when bidding on all levels and types of government contracts.

Despite these shortcomings the FTA is a good deal for Canada. It enhances and protects Canada's access to its major foreign market. It introduces an effective bilateral dispute-settlement mechanism that should eliminate U.S. abuse under its countervail and anti-dumping laws. By these means, the FTA benefits virtually all parts of Canada, from its industrial heartland to its resource-based regions.

It does all this without jeopardizing the major non-economic elements that are the essence of Canada. Except for two relatively modest concessions, Canada's cultural industries were exempted from the agreement. Moreover, Canada's social policies are in no way adversely affected by the FTA. While there was some compromise of Canada's sovereignty in a few areas, the country may have improved on its overall position vis-à-vis its giant neighbor.

The FTA is far superior to any other alternative that is available in terms of Canada's trading relations with the United States. Furthermore, it could provide an encouraging example and precedent for the world and thus help break the logjam that has been holding up a GATT breakthrough and thereby threatening a worldwide trade war. Finally, the FTA provides Canada with a hedge against any such disaster, since it assures Canada of much-improved access to its most important market.

One of the keys to the success of the FTA from a Canadian

point of view stems from the unprecedented effectiveness of the consultative mechanisms that were put in place to advise and counsel the Trade Negotiations Office throughout the negotiations. Canada's able negotiators regularly consulted a host of industry and provincial representatives, and their collective views were reflected in a very meaningful way in the final agreement.

The result is an agreement that Canadians should support. By ensuring Canada more ready and secure access to the U.S. market the FTA will allow this country to realize its full economic potential. In so doing it will enable Canadians to provide more support for their important cultural, regional-development, and social-security programs. The combination will produce both a stronger and more vibrant economy and a more caring and compassionate society.

Conclusions

The challenge is for those who favor the FTA to counter the propaganda campaign being waged against the FTA by refuting it point by point. Beyond this, those who support the FTA must demonstrate their confidence, faith, and trust in the ability of Canadian entrepreneurs and workers to compete successfully in a Canada-U.S. free-trade area. They must also emphasize that only by getting over its unwarranted inferiority complex about its ability to compete in such a broader economic arena can Canada generate the wherewithal to finance the social infrastructure that allows this country to enjoy a justified superiority complex about being a better society.

It will be a shame and a tragedy if the proponents of the FTA allow its detractors to so dishonestly distort its significance for the country's long-run well-being that the FTA somehow goes down to defeat. The FTA is a necessary but not sufficient condition for Canadian prosperity for decades to come. Together with efforts such as those required to contain and reduce the federal deficit, to provide new investment and research and development incentives, and to assist workers adversely affected by necessary changes in society, free trade can provide Canada with the basis for the most soundly based growth and prosperity in its history.

There is an old adage that "the truth shall make you free." In the present context one might well say that "The truth about free trade shall make you a free trader." Certainly if Canadians knew more about the Canada-U.S. FTA many more of them, if indeed not the vast majority, would support it.